IQ
TESTING

IQ TESTING

Increase your vocabulary and develop your powers of calculation and logical reasoning

Philip Carter & Ken Russell

KOGAN PAGE

Publisher's Note

Every possible effort has been made to ensure that the information contained in this book is accurate at the time of going to press, and the publishers and authors cannot accept responsibility for any errors or omissions, however caused. No responsibility for loss or damage occasioned to any person acting, or refraining from action, as a result of the material in this publication can be accepted by the editor, the publisher or any of the authors.

First Indian Edition 2010

Kogan Page India Private Limited
4737/23 Ansari Road,
Daryaganj
New Delhi 110 002

This edition is for sale in Indian subcontinent only. Not for export elsewhere.

ISBN: 978-81-7554-501-4

Published by Vinod Vasishtha for Kogan Page India Private Limited,
4737/23 Ansari Road, Daryaganj, New Delhi - 110 002.

Printed and bound at Raj Press, R-3, Inderpuri, New Delhi - 110 012

Contents

Introduction

The letters IQ stand for Intelligence Quotient. Intelligence can be defined as the ability to respond adaptively to novel situations, while quotient is the number of times that one number will divide into another.

The measured IQ of a child is equal to mental age divided by actual, or chronological, age. For example, if a child of eight years of age obtains a score expected of a ten-year-old, the child will have a measured IQ of 125. This is calculated as follows:

$$\frac{\text{Mental age}}{\text{Chronological age}} \times 100 = \text{IQ}$$

$$\text{Therefore, } \frac{10}{8} \times 100 = 125 \text{ IQ}$$

This method of calculating IQ does not apply to adults because beyond the age of 18 there is little or no change in mental development. Adults, therefore, have to be judged on an IQ test in which the average score is 100. The results are graded above and below this norm according to known test scores.

The tests that have been specially compiled for this book have not been standardised, so an actual IQ assessment cannot be given. However, at the end of this section there is a guide to assessing your performance, and there is also a cumulative score for performance on all ten tests.

The tests in this book are intended as valuable practice for readers who may have to take an IQ test in the future, and they are also designed to increase readers' powers of vocabulary and to develop their powers of calculation and logical reasoning.

The book consists of ten separate tests for you to attempt, each of 40 questions. Each test is of approximately the same degree of difficulty.

A time limit of **90 minutes** is allowed for each test. The correct answers are given at the end of the book, and you should award yourself one point for each correct answer.

Use the following table to assess your performance:

One test:

Score	*Rating*
36–40	exceptional
31–35	excellent
25–30	very good
19–24	good
14–18	average

Ten tests:

Score	*Rating*
351–400	exceptional
301–350	excellent
241–300	very good
181–240	good
140–180	average

Test one

1

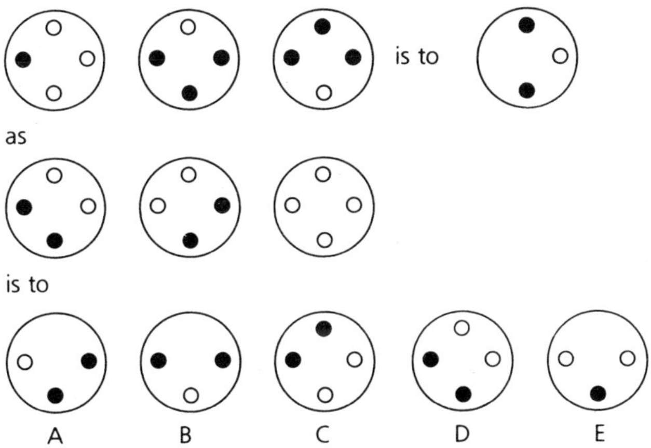

2 Which is the odd one out?

FIRTH, ESPLANADE, SOUND, MAIN, FJORD

3 What number should replace the question marks?

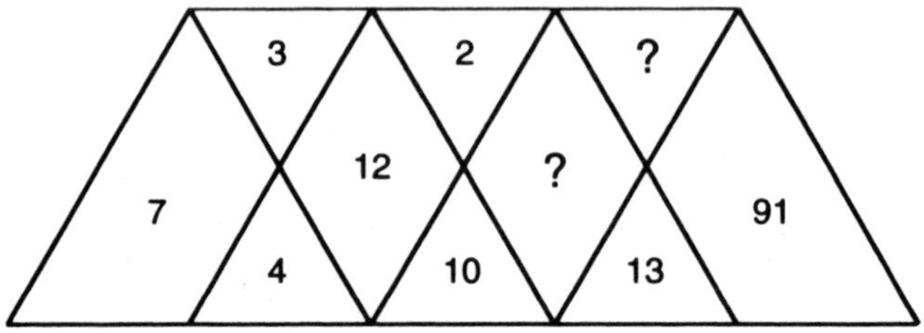

4 ANODE, ALTO, NEEDLE

Which word comes next?

YIELD, LAND, DEALT, TEND, FIRM, TANDEM

5

Which option should replace the question mark?

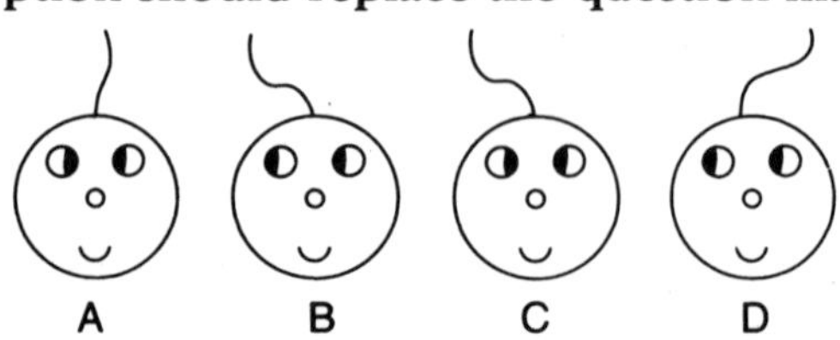

A B C D

6 483 : 144 : 56
257 : 175 : 85
139 : 117 : ?

7 Eight synonyms of the keyword MODESTY are shown. Take one letter from each of these synonyms in turn to spell out a further synonym of MODESTY.

shyness, bashfulness, meekness, timidity, simplicity, diffidence, propriety, coyness

8 Find the starting point and find a 16-letter phrase (3,4,5,4) reading clockwise. Only alternate letters are shown.

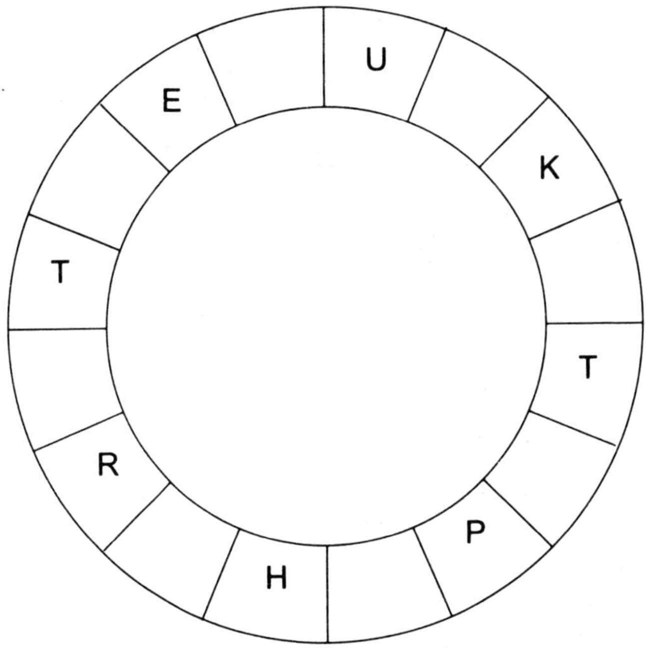

9 megalomania: power
hedomania: a) religion
b) talking
c) work
d) pleasure
e) travelling

10 What is PROSELYTE?
a) a protective substance
b) an instrument used to measure angles
c) a short wooden supporting beam
d) a person converted to a religion
e) a wet-and-dry-bulb thermometer

11 Insert two letters into each bracket so that they finish the words on the left and start the words on the right. The letters inserted should spell out a six-letter word when read downwards in pairs.

PA (**) UN
MO (**) AL
BR (**) IT

12 What numbers should replace the question marks?

4	8	7	6	2	5	4	8
5	7	8	2	6	4	5	7
2	6	4	5	7	8	2	6
6	2	5	4	?	?	6	2
7	5	2	8	?	?	7	5
8	4	6	7	5	2	8	4
4	8	7	6	2	5	4	8

13 Which is the odd one out?

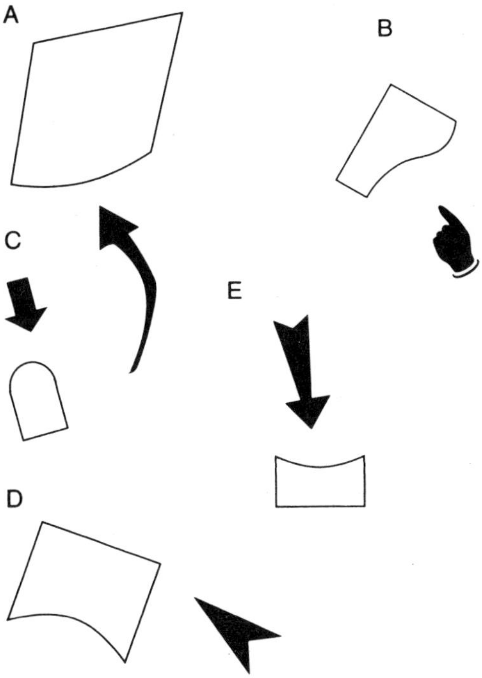

14 What number should replace the question mark?

4	7	9	6	3	6	8	5
2	3	7	1	3	4	8	2
9	6	3	5	8	5	2	?

15 A B C D E F G H

What letter is two to the right of the letter immediately to the left of the letter three to the right of the letter immediately to the left of the letter C?

16

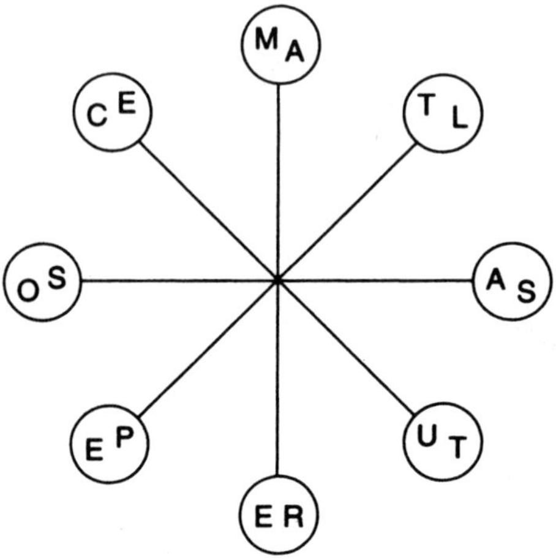

Take just one letter from each circle and, reading clockwise, spell out an eight-letter word meaning INTENSIFY. You have to find the starting point.

17

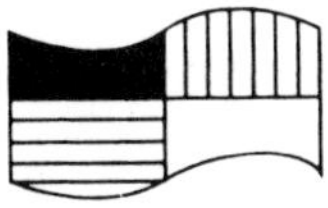

is to

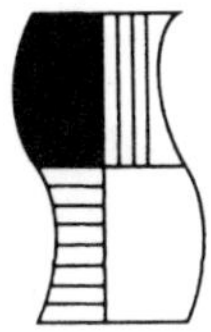

as

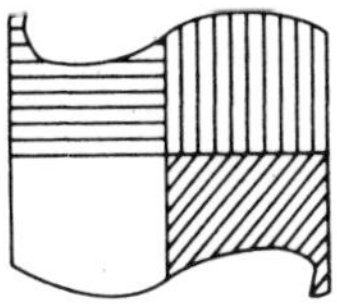

is to

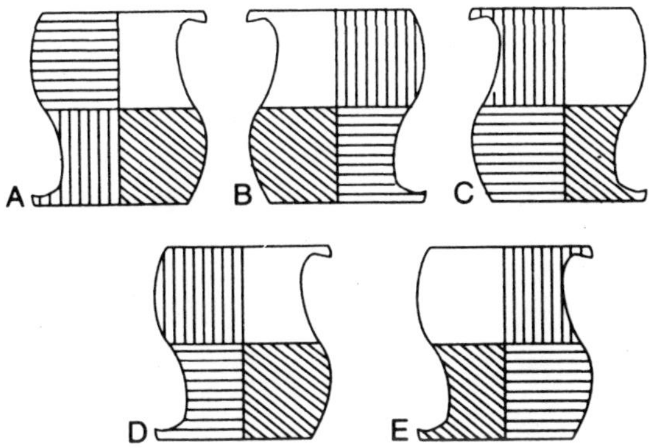

18 Only one set of letters below can be rearranged into a five-letter English word. Can you find the word?

NURDL
KIRDO
NEOPL
MIRBA
MERCA
TONAM

19 Which two words are opposite in meaning?

MORTIFIED, VERITABLE, PENITENT, PLEASANT, REMORSELESS, RASH

20 ICONOCLASTIC is to anti-establishment as WITHERSHINS is to:

a) ANTI-CLIMAX
b) ANTI-INTELLECTUAL
c) ANTI-SOCIAL
d) ANTI-PROGRESSIVE
e) ANTI-CLOCKWISE

21 Which word means the same as HARPING?

a) GRATIFYING
b) UNFEELING
c) BENEFITING
d) BEGINNING
e) REITERATION

22 Using only these five letters make a seven-letter word.

O E

L

R F

23 Place two four-letter bits together to make an eight-letter word which is a REPTILE.

ANAG	SEUR	TERR	ASEN	LISK
INDA	MOCC	BASI	DINO	APON

24 Find a one-word anagram of:

CARTHORSE

CLUE: It is musical

25 Find a ten-letter word by moving from circle to circle in any direction, but only use each circle once.

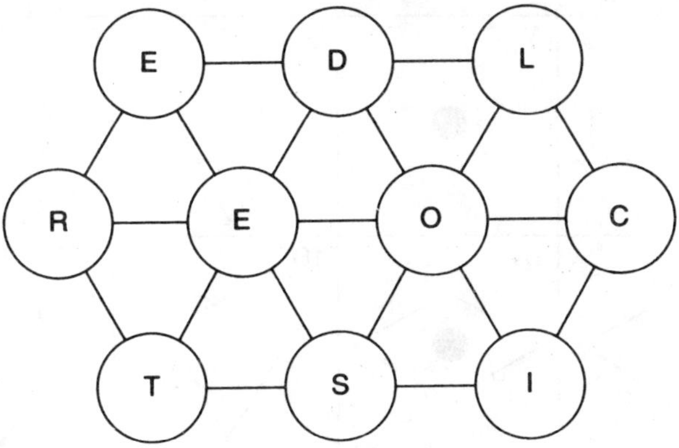

26 Fill in the blanks to find an eight-letter animal. You may move either clockwise or anticlockwise.

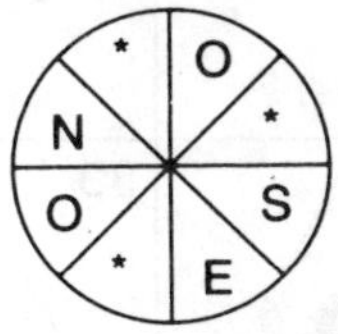

27 Each of the nine squares in the grid marked 1A to 3C should incorporate all the lines and symbols which are shown in the squares of the same letter and number immediately above and to the left. For example, 2B should incorporate all the lines and symbols that are in 2 and B.

One of the squares is incorrect. Which one is it?

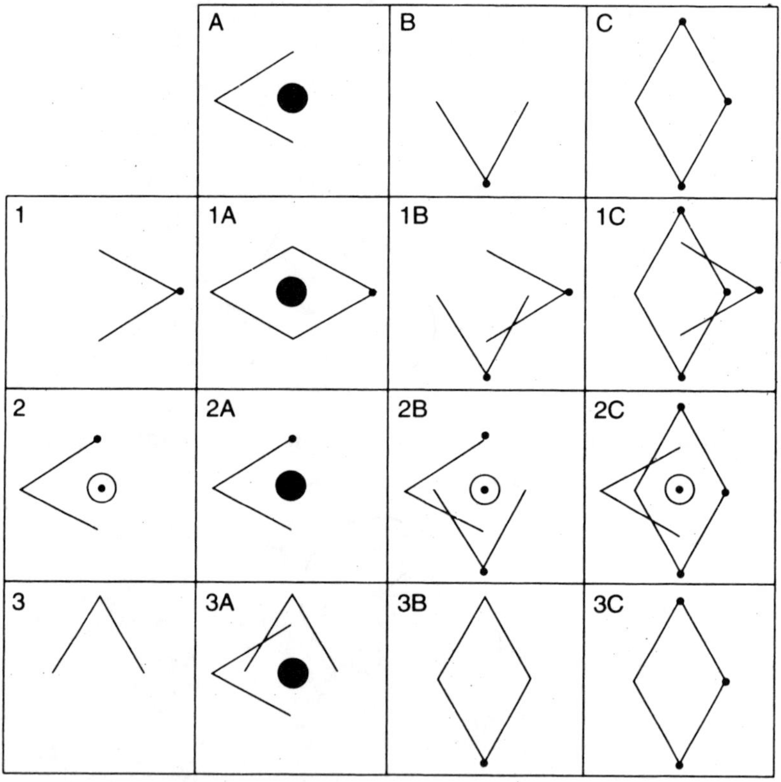

28 What is the meaning of CHAGRIN?

a) DELIGHT
b) VEXATION
c) MEDIOCRITY
d) SURPRISE

29 Make two 6-letter SHIPS from these 12 letters.

A E E G G H L L R R U W

W . . . . .
L . . . . .

30 What number should replace the question mark?

1, 30, 8, 24, 15, 18, 22, ?

31 Which two words mean the opposite?

FRIGHTFUL, FEASIBLE, GHASTLY, SCHEMING, HINDERED, DUCTILE, TRITENESS, IMPRACTICABLE

32 Find a 12-letter word by starting at a corner and working towards the centre in a spiral.

E	X	P
E	S	L
N	S	I
T	I	C

33 What number should replace the question mark?

6	14	5	4
8	4	2	6
9	16	5	5
7	7	2	7
4	4	1	?

34 Find the order, to slide 1-2-3 into A-B-C so as to make three eight-letter words.

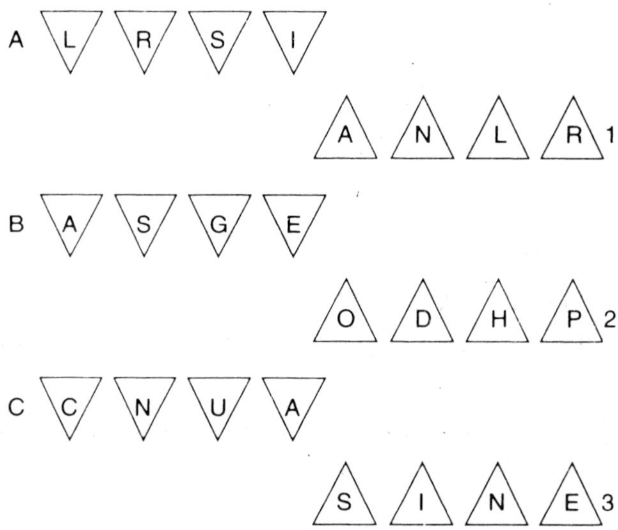

35 Find this ten-letter legal term.

. E . L . G . N . E

36 Find three islands.

a) . A . A . A . O .
b) . A . H . T . A .
c) . A . T . C . E .

37 What fraction generates this recurring decimal?

.123777

38 Simplify

$16 - 9 \times 2 + 5 \div 2$

39 Find a 16-letter English county by going into each room once.

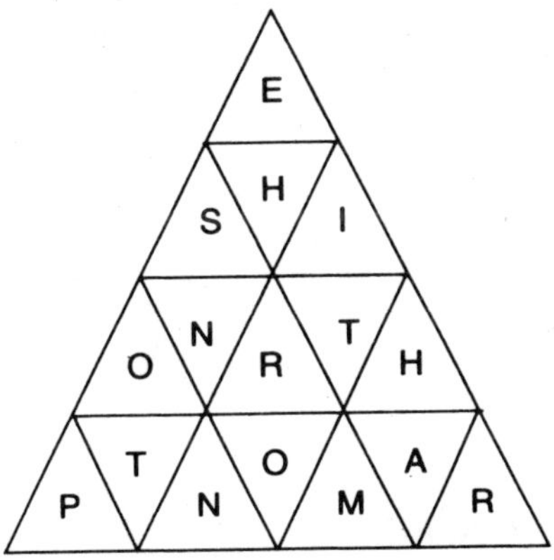

40 Fill in the blanks to find two words that are synonyms. You may move either clockwise or anticlockwise.

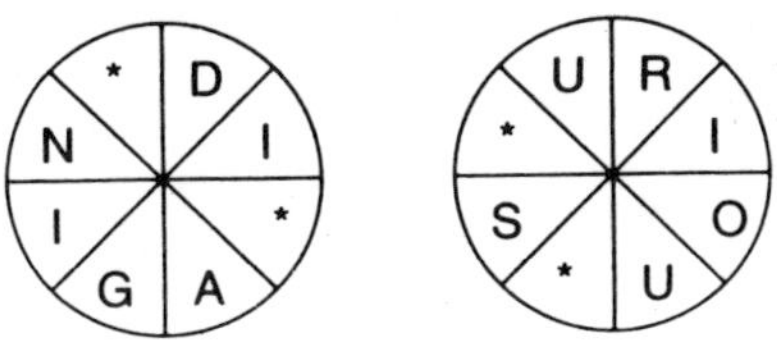

Test two

1

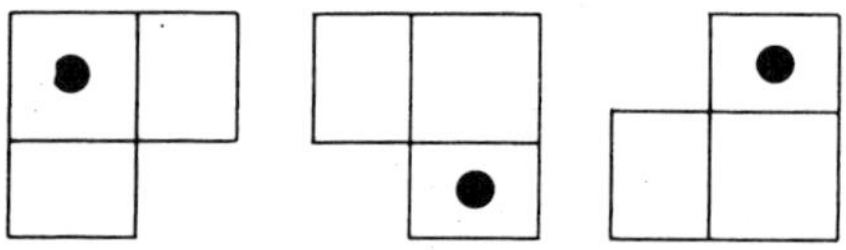

What comes next in the above sequence?

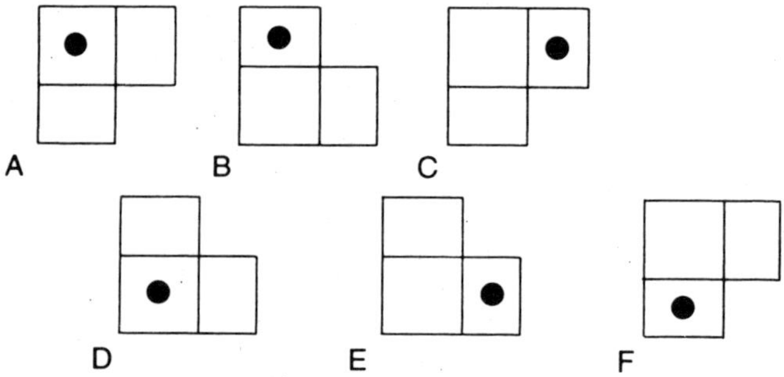

2 What is AMORPHOUS?

a) SHAPELESS
b) LOVING
c) CHARMING
d) SELECTIVE
e) REPETITIVE

3 What numbers should replace the question marks?

1	2	3	4
3	7	15	?
7	23	63	?
15	71	255	?

4 FUSE is to SOLDER as TEMPER is to:
ENCASE, EXPAND, WELD, HAMMER, ANNEAL

5

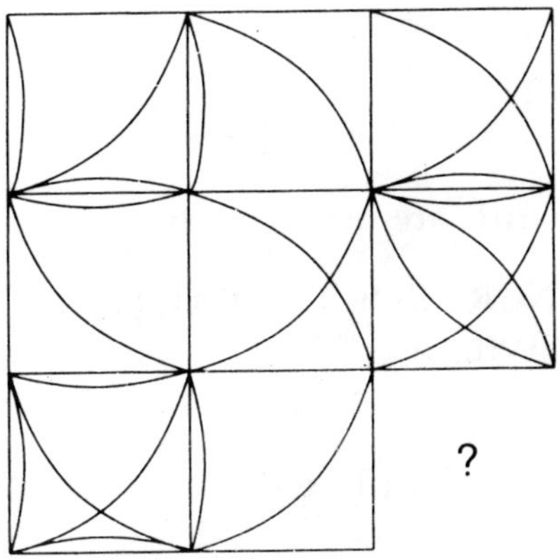

Which option below should replace the question mark?

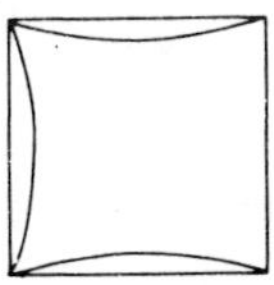
A

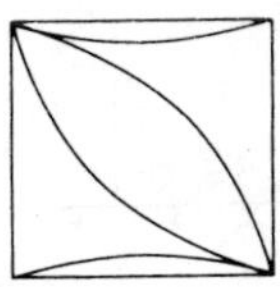
B

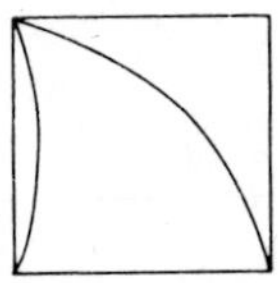
C

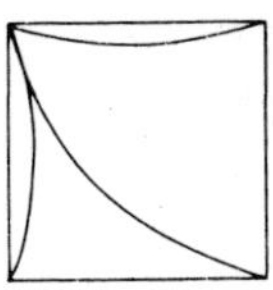
D

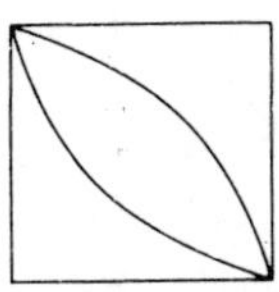
E

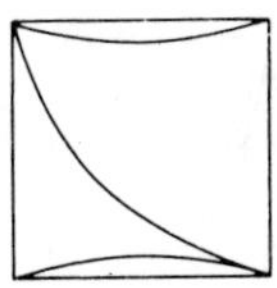
F

6 What number should replace the question mark?

945 (76) 374
384 (222) 162
965 (?) 324

7 Start at one of the corner letters and spiral clockwise round the perimeter to spell out a nine-letter word, finishing at the central letter. You have to provide the missing letters.

*	L	R
C	E	E
N	O	*

8 Which two words are most nearly opposite in meaning?

ELEGANT, UNGRACIOUS, HOSTILE, INDISCREET, NEGATIVE, CIVIL

9 What letter should replace the question mark?

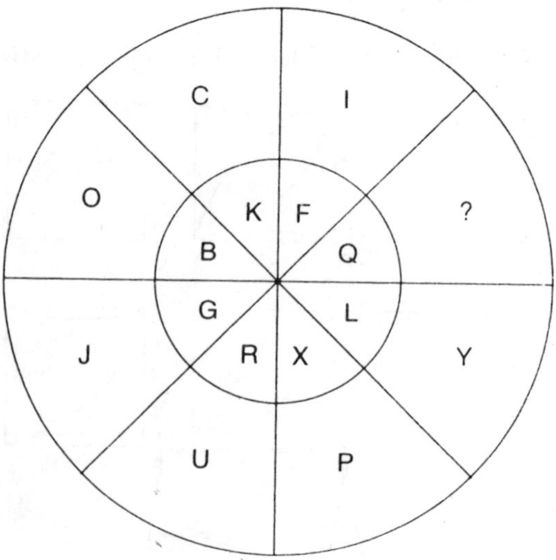

10 NOISE RARITY is an anagram of which two words that are synonyms (5, 6)?

11

Which two symbols come next in the above sequence?

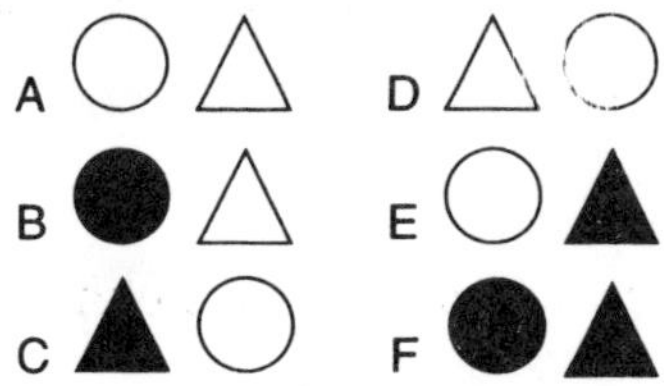

12 What number should replace the question mark?

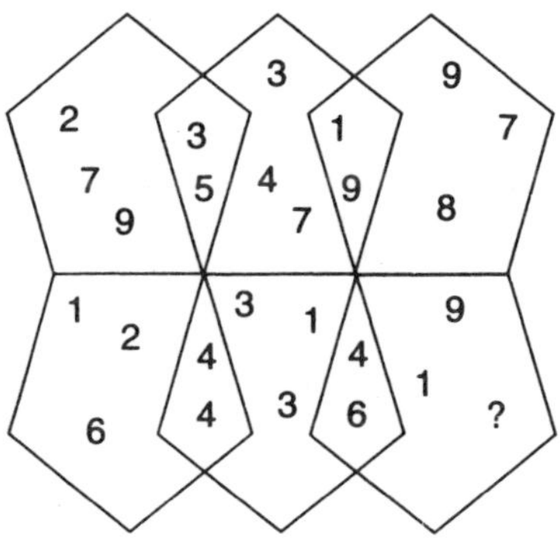

13 Which of the following is not an anagram of a country?

old pan
big mule
cool van
any row
hay rung

14 Sunday, Monday, Tuesday, Wednesday, Thursday, Friday, Saturday

Which day comes immediately after the day which comes three days before the day which comes immediately after the day which comes three days before Friday?

15 ED, GE, OW, EN, UE, GO, ?

Which two letters complete the above sequence?

ET, AN, VE, CH, ON

16 Which two words are closest in meaning?

PERTAIN, ALARM, APPLY, EXAMINE, COAX, EMBODY

17

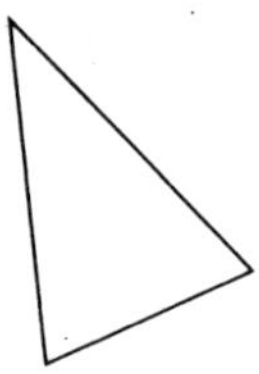

is to

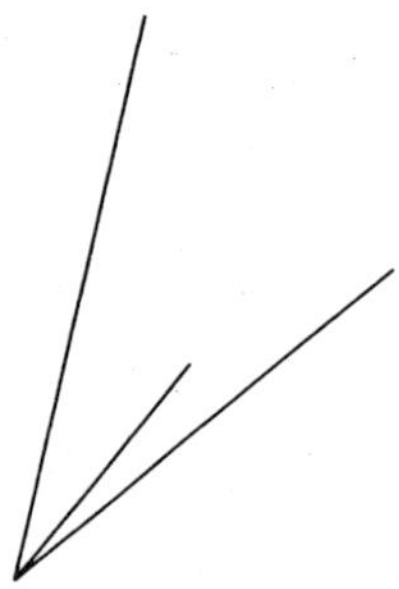

as

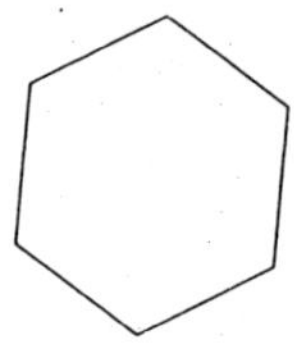

is to:

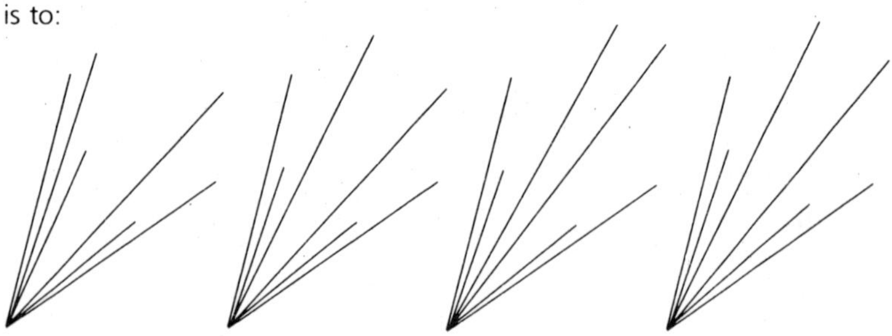

A B C D

18 What do these words have in common?

REMARKABLE, GIGANTIC, PORTUGAL, BRIGADIER

19 Change one letter only in each word to produce a familiar phrase.

slim if tie men

20

20	16	25	29	12
5	8	28	7	11
32	31	18	30	4
26	14	27	6	10
9	22	19	3	21
15	13	1	17	2

Which number is three places away from itself plus 2, two places away from itself less 1, three places away from itself less 4 and two places away from itself plus 1?

21 Find this ten-letter artistic word.

. A . I . A . U . E

22 Change $^{10}/_{13}$ to a decimal to 4 places.

23 Find a six-letter word using only these four letters.

X A
T I

24 Find three celebrities from different generations.

a) M . D . N . A
b) . A . R . A . K .
c) . T . E . S . N .

25 Place eight of these pairs of letters together to make two eight-letter words. One pair is not used.

HT	VE	IG
VI	EY	BI
LO	RD	ES

26 Replace the blanks and find two words which are synonyms. You may move either clockwise or anticlockwise.

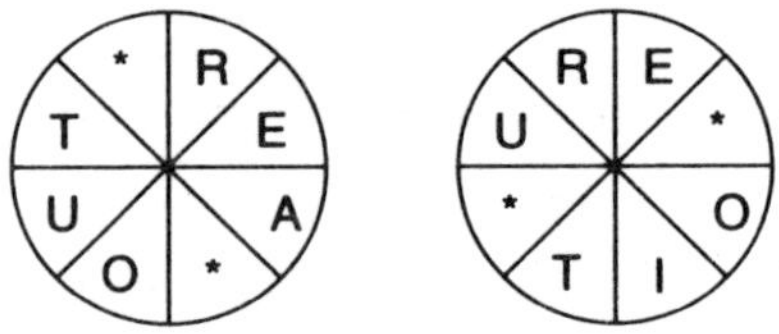

27

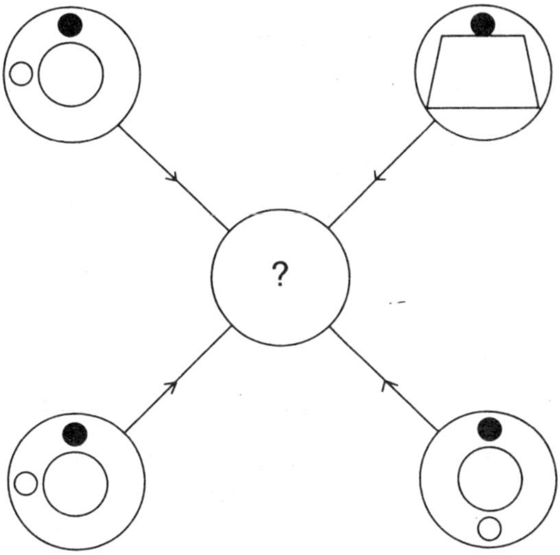

Each line and symbol which appears in the four outer circles, above, is transferred to the centre circle according to these rules:

If a line or symbol occurs in the outer circles:

Once: it is transferred
Twice: it is possibly transferred
Three times: it is transferred
Four times: it is not transferred

Which of the circles shown below should appear at the centre of the diagram, above?

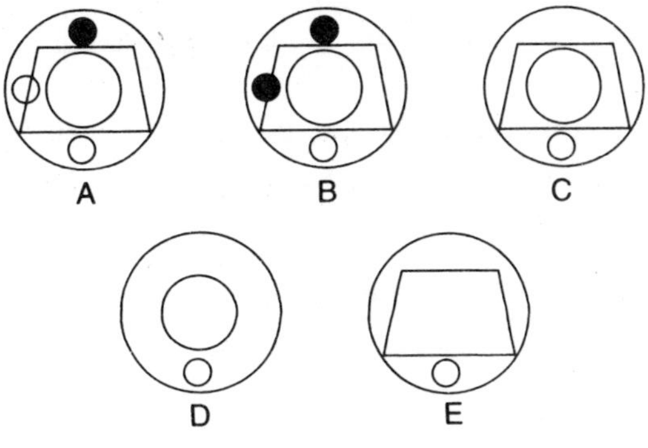

28 Find a ten-letter word which is used in medicine.

H . O . O . O . M

29 Place two sets of three letters together to equal a six-letter dog.

BEA BAR LIE SAL POO
BED DEL UKE COL DIE

30 Which word means the opposite of RISIBLE?

a) RIOTOUS c) RIDICULOUS e) SERIOUS
b) CONFUSING d) RIGHTFUL

31 Make two six-letter nautical terms from these twelve letters.

A A C F H H M N O O R T

F . . . . .
A . . . . .

32 Rearrange the words to find a trite saying.

GET	THAT	COMMITTEES	IN
COMPUTERS	TOO	WE	THEM
THEM	ORGANISE	CAN	IF
WILL	INTO	POWERFUL	DO

33 After arranging, three of the contents of the circles will make a six-letter word, but one will not. Which one?

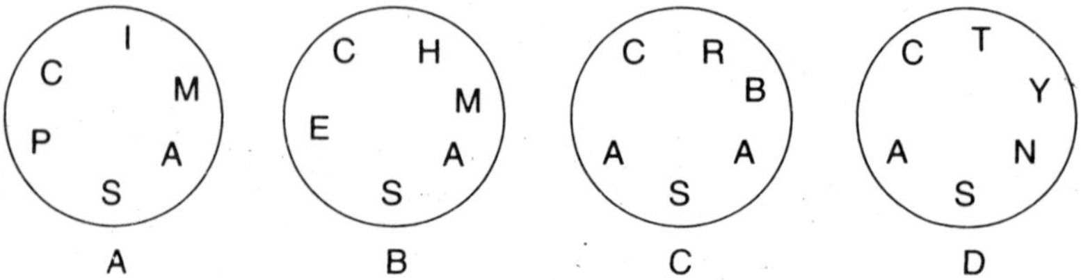

34 Each of the nine squares in the grid marked 1A to 3C should incorporate all the lines and symbols which are shown in the squares of the same letter and number immediately above and to the left. For example, 2B should incorporate all the lines and symbols that are in 2 and B.

One of the squares is incorrect. Which one is it?

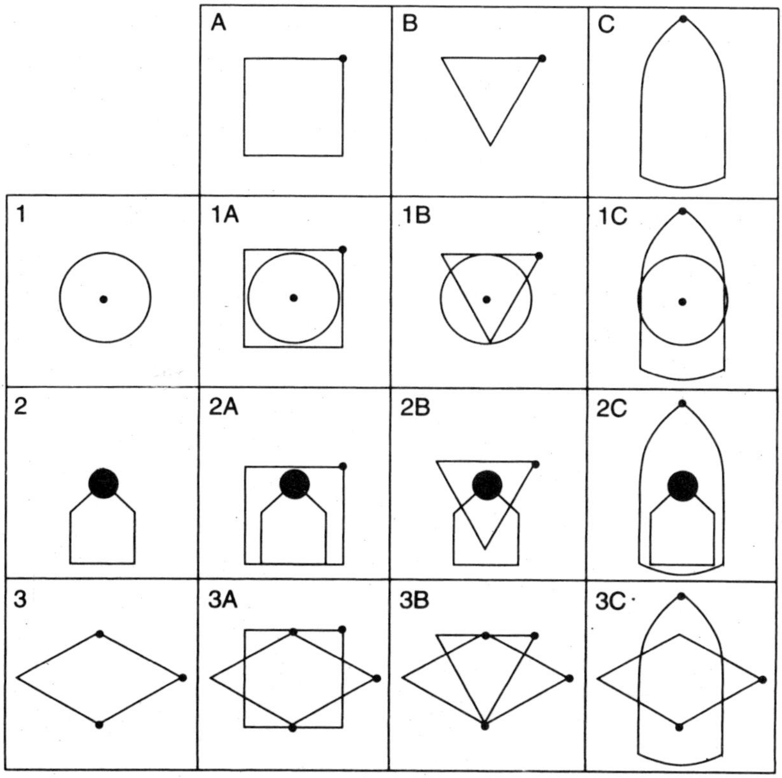

35 What is a CLARENCE?

a) a dinner party
b) a butler
c) a kitchen maid
d) a four-wheeled carriage

36 What is the name given to a group of curs?

a) COWARDICE
b) CLUSTER
c) COLLECTION
d) CONVOCATION

37 What number should replace the question mark?

$2\frac{1}{2}$, 12, $3\frac{3}{4}$, $9\frac{1}{4}$, 5, $6\frac{1}{2}$, $6\frac{1}{4}$, ?

38 Find a one-word anagram of:

NAY I REPENT IT

CLUE: Contains prisoners

39 Find an eight-letter word by making three-letter words.

G	S	M	S	O	T	P	R
U	P	A	K	F	O	A	E
*	*	*	*	*	*	*	*

40 Find these two nine-letter words that are insects. Place the letters in the grid.

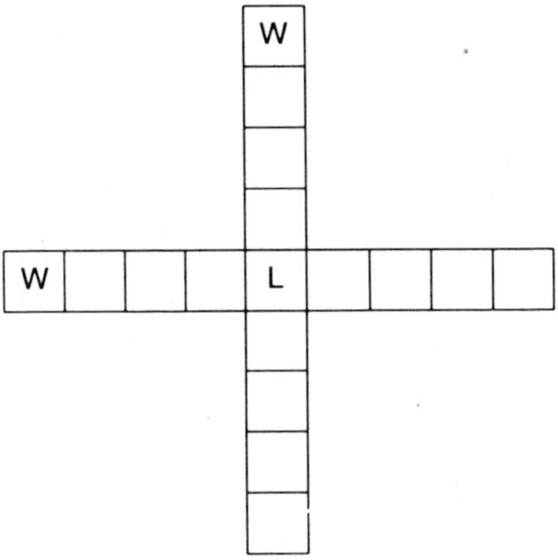

A O
B O
D O
E R
E S
F U
L Y

Test three

1 DILEMMA is to QUANDARY as IMPASSE is to:

a) STALEMATE
b) IMBROGLIO
c) PROBLEM
d) MORASS
e) ENIGMA

2 Which number should replace the question mark?

97	25	4	6	3	81
82					74
16					2
?					53
34	1	7	28	5	69

3 Find the starting point and find a 16-letter phrase (2,6,8) reading clockwise. Only alternate letters are shown.

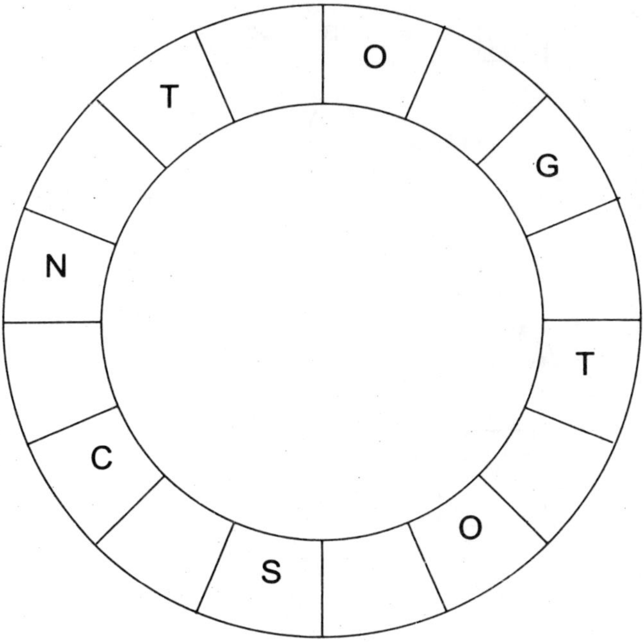

4 3664 : 68
2581 : 59
1649 : ?

5 Which is the odd one out?

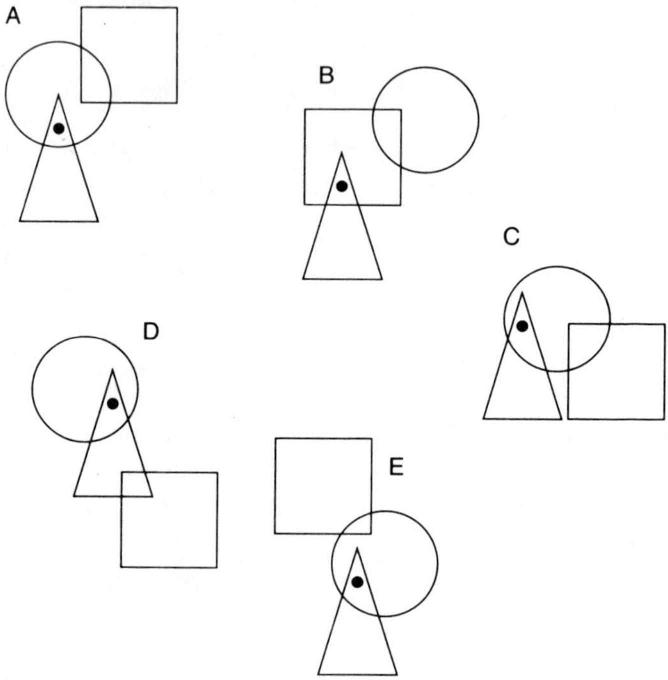

6 If an African country within another African country (4 in 7) is SO(MALI)A, can you find a Middle Eastern country in an East European country?

7 Which is the odd one out?

PEW, FONT, NAVE, BELFRY, ALTAR

8 Which two words are closest in meaning?

SEEDY, SORRY, SOPORIFIC, GLOOMY, SLEEPY, SENTIMENTAL

9 Which is the odd one out?

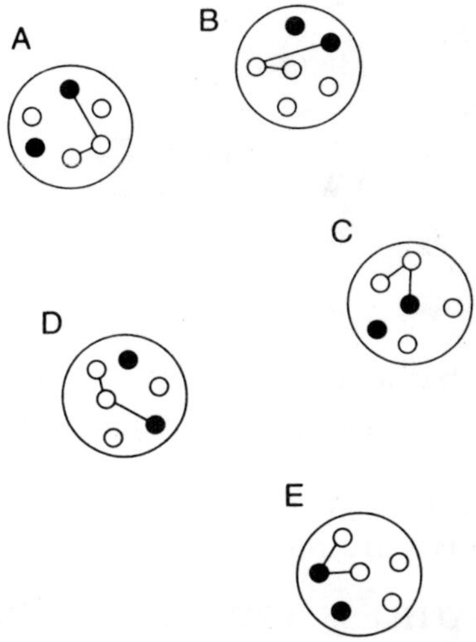

10 What number should replace the question mark?

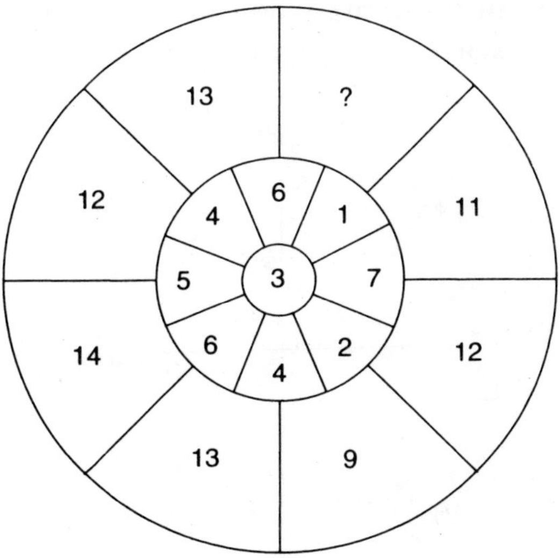

11

ABC	DEF	GHI
1	2	3
JKL	MNO	PQR
4	5	6
STU	VWX	YZ
7	8	9
*	0	#

Each number has a choice of letters.
Dial an American president: 365826 142824152

12 Which two words are most nearly opposite in meaning?

ETHICAL, DEATHLESS, EPHEMERAL, EXALTED, AFFABLE, WANTON

13 Find two words that are synonyms reading clockwise. Each word starts at a different circle and all letters are used.

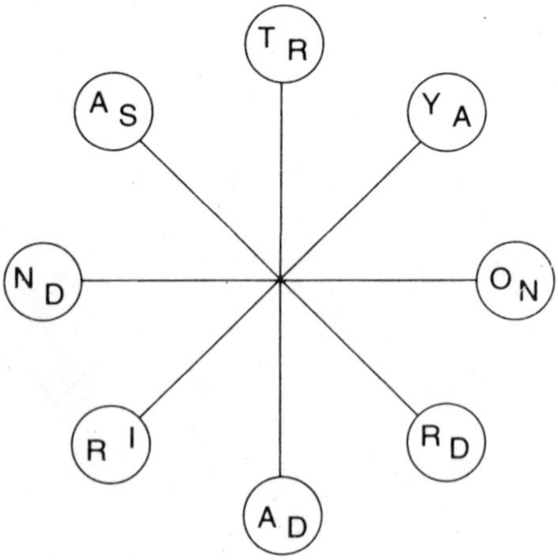

14 Add one letter, not necessarily the same letter, to each word at the front, end or middle, to find two words that are opposite in meaning.

MASH SWAP

15 Which is the odd one out?

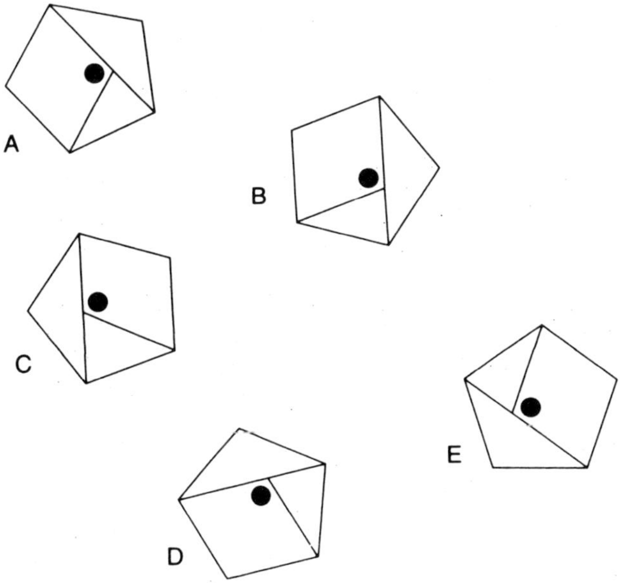

16 What number should replace the question mark?

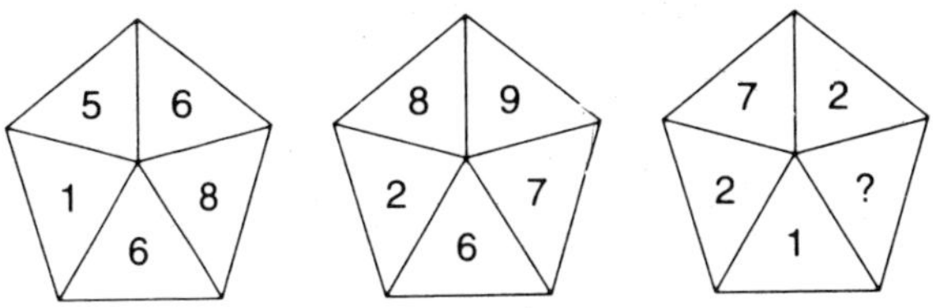

17 EQUINE is to HORSE as LEPORINE is to:

a) HARE
b) LEOPARD
c) DEER
d) RAT
e) WOLF

18 Which letter should replace the question mark?

A	B		B	A		S	F
C	D		R	I		A	V
E	F		N	L		T	E
F	I		T	D		Y	?

19 Insert the letters provided into each quadrant to form two words of a phrase, both reading clockwise, one around the inner circle and one around the outer circle.

NE : LAMP
SE : TEUP
SW : SERR
NW: OONC

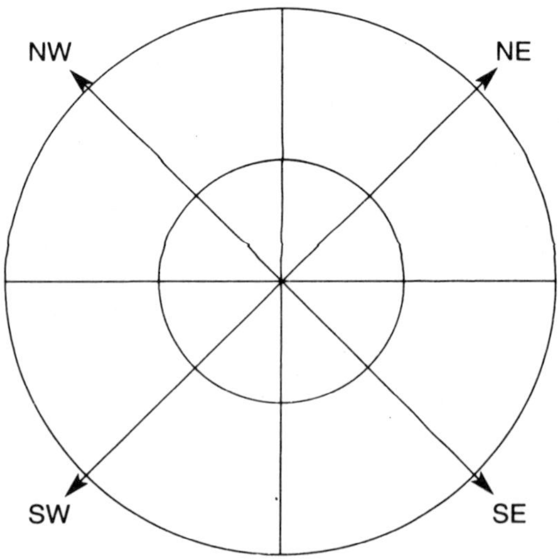

20

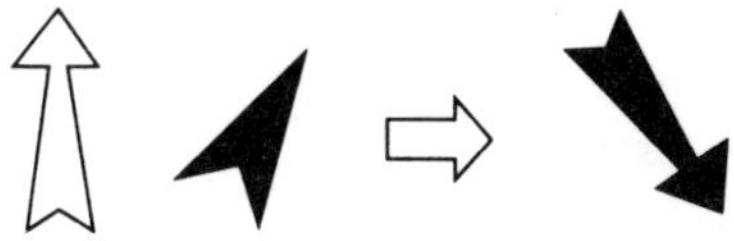

What comes next in the above sequence?

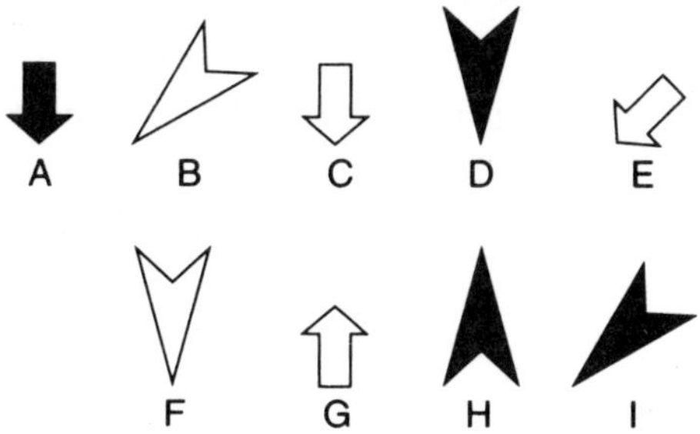

21 Simplify

$$\frac{1260}{2340}$$

22 Which word means the same as FLACCID?

a) CAPRICIOUS
b) MUDDLED
c) FLABBY
d) FITFUL
e) FERTILE

23 Using only these five letters make a seven-letter word.

G P

A

R E

24 Which two words mean the opposite?

ENDEAVOUR, SELECTED, ELECTRIFY, TRANQUILLISE, NONPLUSSED, WHIMSICAL

25 Fill in the blanks to find two words which are antonyms. You may move clockwise or anticlockwise.

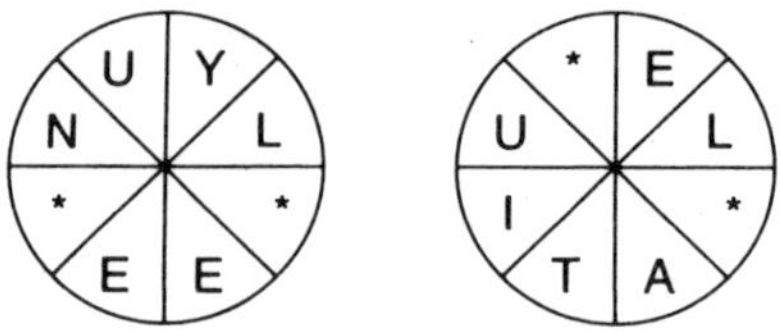

26 Find a ten-letter word by moving from circle to circle. Each letter may be used once only.

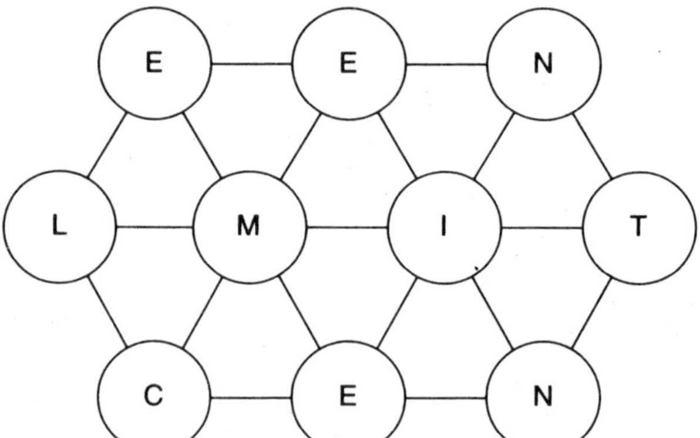

27 Where should the letters C O K E go – above or below the line?

A N T V X F Y H I W Z L M

B P D Q R G S U J

28 COVEN is to WITCHES as CLAMOUR is to

a) WIDGEON
b) MOLES
c) ROOKS
d) HERON
e) BADGERS

29 Make two six-letter weapons out of these twelve letters.

A B C D E E G L N S T U

B . . . . .
C . . . . .

30 Place two four-letter bits together to equal an eight-letter word which is a food.

FLAP	GOUL	BECH	LINN	IGES
ASHE	DUMP	JACC	PORR	AMEL

31 The vowels have been omitted from this trite saying. See if you can replace them.

FMBTN DSNTH RTYHV NTGTT

32 Find a twelve-letter word by starting at a corner and working towards the centre in a spiral.

R	H	T
O	R	E
W	E	M
F	L	A

33 Fill in the blanks to find two words which are antonyms. You may move clockwise or anticlockwise.

34 Find a ten-letter word by travelling along the lines.

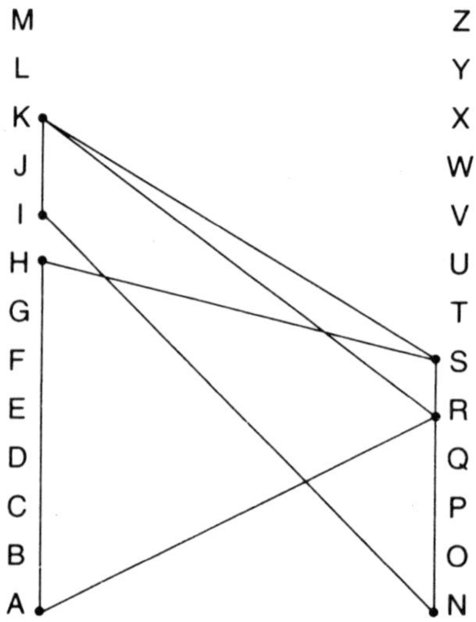

35 What colour is CORNELIAN?

a) GREEN
b) BLUE
c) RED
d) YELLOW

36 Place two three-letter bits together to make a fish.

KIP	NOW	CON	BLE	BAR
DER	GEL	MIN	PEN	

37 What is the meaning of the word COMPITAL?

a) pertaining to CROSSROADS
b) pertaining to DOCTORS
c) pertaining to VIADUCTS
d) pertaining to CHIMNEY SWEEPS

38 Find this ten-letter musical term:

. I . I . U . N . O

39 Place eight of these pairs of letters together to make two eight-letter words. One pair is not used.

NG	LL	IP
WE	KI	JE
ER	SH	SO

40 What number should replace the question mark?

9	3	2	1
24	2	6	6
21	3	4	3
18	3	4	2
20	5	1	?

Test four

1 What letter should replace the question mark?

A	I		M	U		Y	G
C	G		O	S		?	E

2 Which is the odd one out?

COGENT, COMPELLING, EMPIRICAL, INCISIVE, TRENCHANT

3 GUSTO is to VIVACITY as ELAN is to:

a) JOIE DE VIVRE
b) ENJOYMENT
c) DASH
d) LIVELINESS
e) VITALITY

4 What number should replace the question mark?

3	6	2	8
2	1	1	3
1	3	1	4
5	5	3	?

5

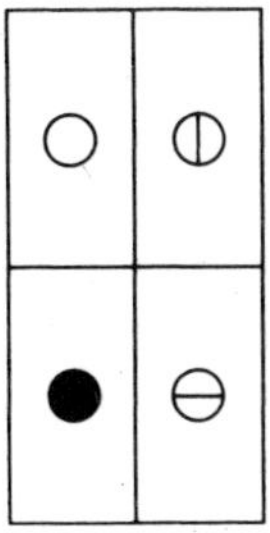

is to

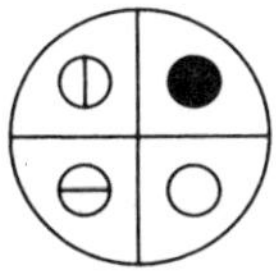

as

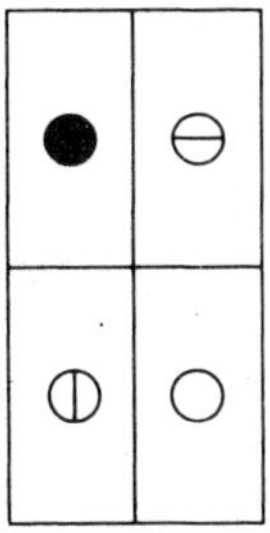

is to

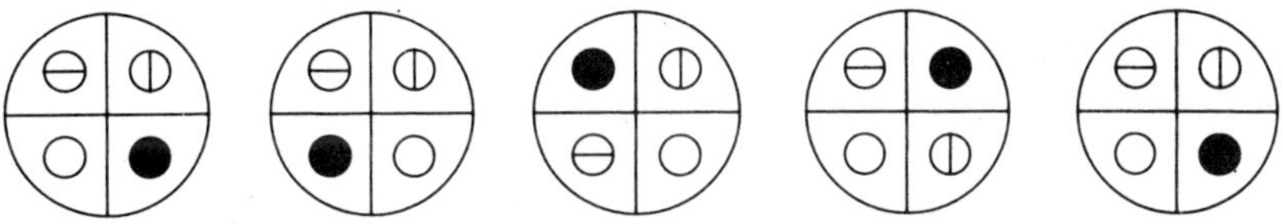

A B C D E

6 What number should replace the question mark?

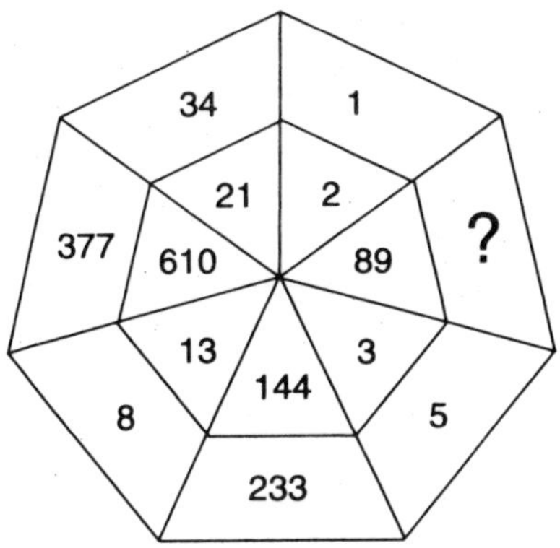

7 Which two words are closest in meaning?

GLEE, GAINSAY, DISCOURAGE, BENEFIT, CONTRADICT, HOPE

8 Work from letter to adjacent letter horizontally and vertically, but not diagonally, to spell out a twelve-letter word. You must find the starting point and fill in the missing letters.

T	S	S	C
*	I	E	A
O	*	O	*

9 Which word in brackets is most nearly opposite in meaning to the word in capitals?

ERUDITE (amiss, uninformed, young, rambling, ambiguous)

10 What is the longest word that can be produced from the following ten letters?

MURDPOBCAH

11

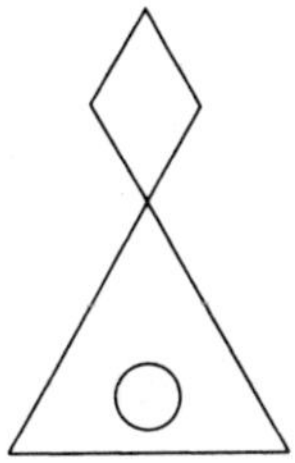

is to

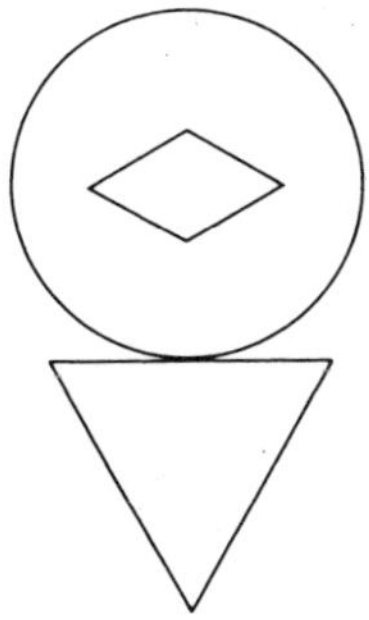

as

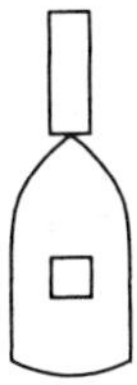

is to

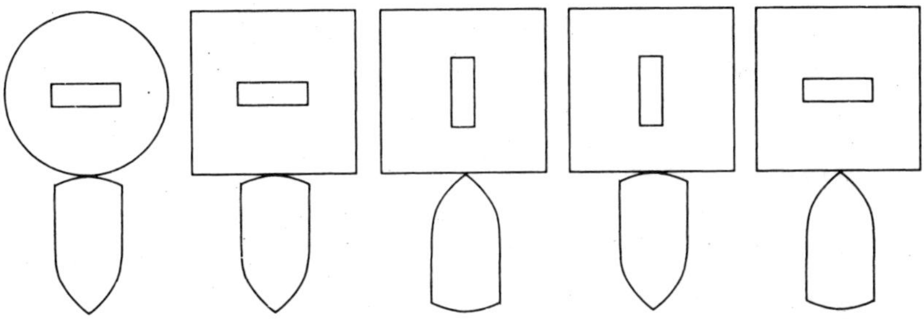

A B C D E

12 What number should replace the question mark?

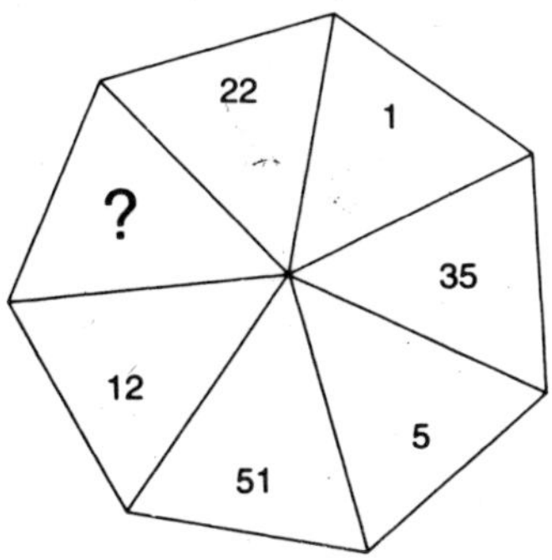

13 What is the missing letter?

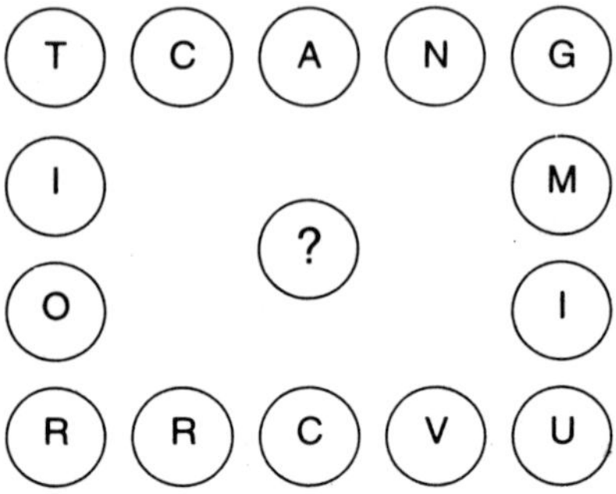

14 Solve the clues to find four six-letter words. The same three letters are represented by XYZ in each word.

XYZ * * *	bodily vessel
* XYZ * *	split
* * XYZ *	floor of a fireplace
* * * XYZ	outwit

15 4135792 : 9753142

3682417 : 7318642

9172843 : ?

16 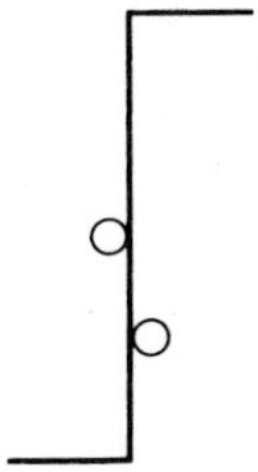

is to

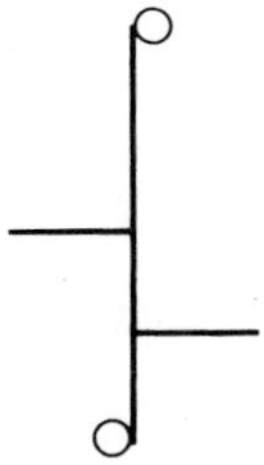

as

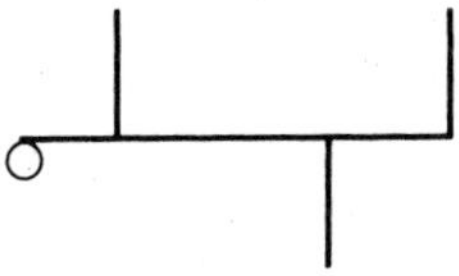

is to

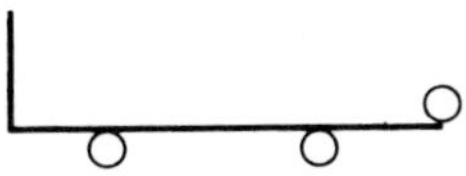

A

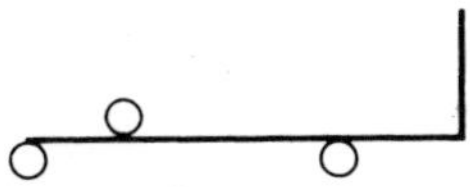

B

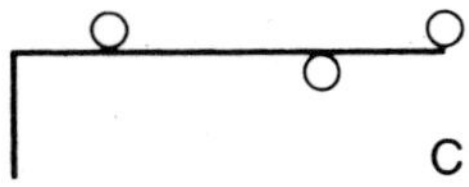

C

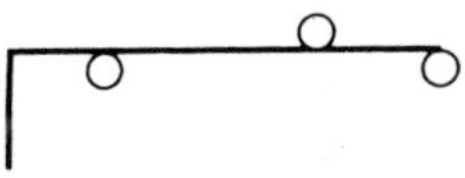

D

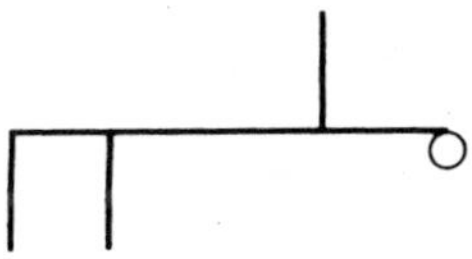

E

17 Insert a word that means the same as the definitions outside the brackets.

to fall behind ( ) to cover a pipe

18 Which two words that sound alike but are spelled differently mean:

discharge/inclined channel

19 Insert the missing consonants to form a magic word square in which all five words can be read both across and down.

D N S L
N T T R
R S T
T D

	A		E	
A		O		E
	O	A		
E			U	E
	E		E	

20

What comes next in the above sequence?

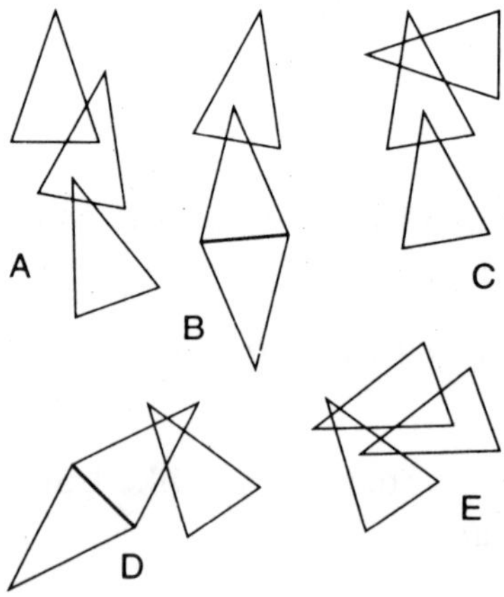

21 What is the name given to a group of wild fowl?

a) PARTY
b) PACK
c) PLUMP
d) PACE

22 Find a six-letter word using only these four letters.

Y	O
G	L

23 Which anagram below is not a building term?

a) LOAPUC
b) RAGETR
c) TARKEA
d) THINLP
e) RIDREG

24 Which word is the opposite of OCCULT?

a) NATURAL
b) LATENT
c) PERIL
d) CORPOREAL
e) WEIRD

25 Place eight of these pairs of letters together to make two eight-letter words. One pair of letters is not used.

YP	RD	LI
LY	LO	BI
OP	RE	LL

26 Fill in the blanks to find an eight-letter fish. You may move clockwise or anticlockwise.

27

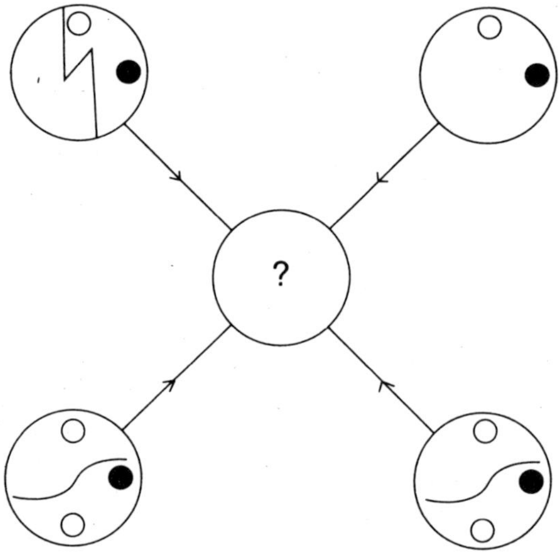

Each line and symbol which appears in the four outer circles, above is transferred to the centre circle according to these rules:

If a line or symbol occurs in the outer circles:

Once: it is transferred
Twice: it is possibly transferred
Three times: it is transferred
Four times: it is not transferred

Which of the circles shown below should appear at the centre of the diagram, on page 48?

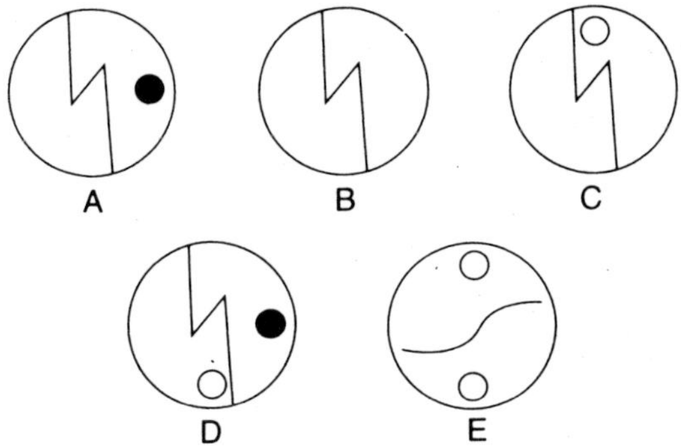

28 Simplify

$$\frac{1470}{1680}$$

29 Place two 3-letter bits together to make a six-letter word which is a flower.

VIA	VIO	BEG	PAN
SAL	ONA	SIE	LEY

30 Make two 6-letter tools out of these twelve letters.

C E E G H I I L L M S T

C . . . . .
G . . . . .

31 Find a ten-letter word which is a medical term.

. I . G . V . T . S

32 Which word when placed in front of these words makes new words?

LET
ROAD
(. . . .) FENCE
MASTER
TAIL

33 After arranging, three of the contents of the circles will make a six-letter word, but one will not. Which one?

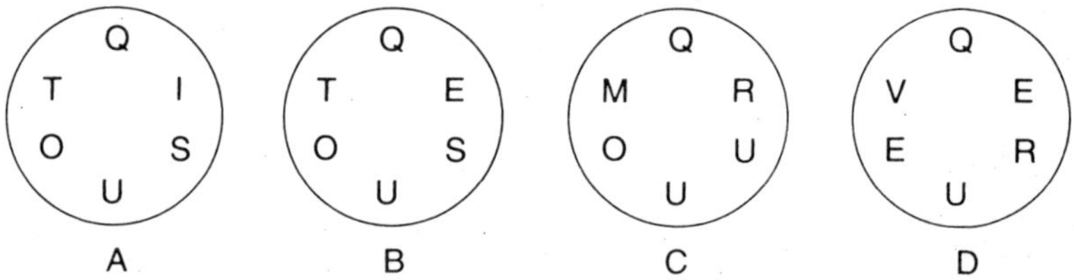

34 Which of these collections of pipes can carry the greatest volume of water?

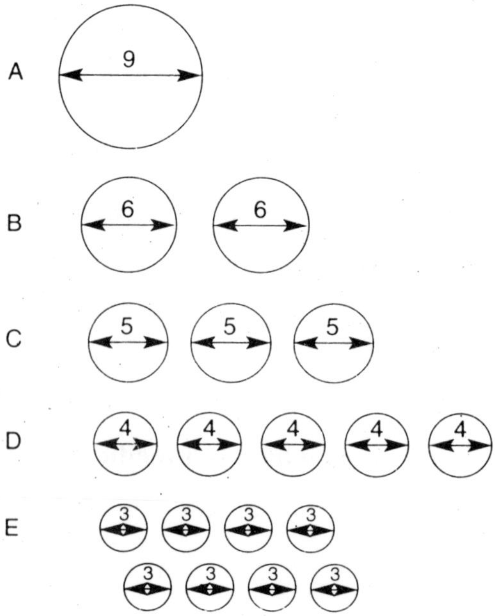

35 Find three animals.

. H . C . A . E .
. U . F . L .
. A . I .

36 What is the meaning of RAILLERY?

a) PERT SPEECH
b) BENEVOLENCE
c) SUPPORT
d) SALIENT

37 Which number should replace the question mark?

2.2, 6.1, 3.1, 5.2, 4.0, 4.3, 4.9, ?

38 Change $\frac{80}{150}$ to a decimal to 5 decimal places.

39 Rearrange the words to find a trite saying.

LONG	IS	LIFE	SHORTNESS
OF	ONLY	THE	TO
WEAR	TO	FACE	THE
COMPENSATE	FOR	A	WAY

40 What number should replace the question mark?

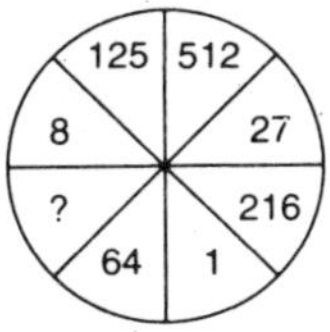

Test five

1 How many lines appear below?

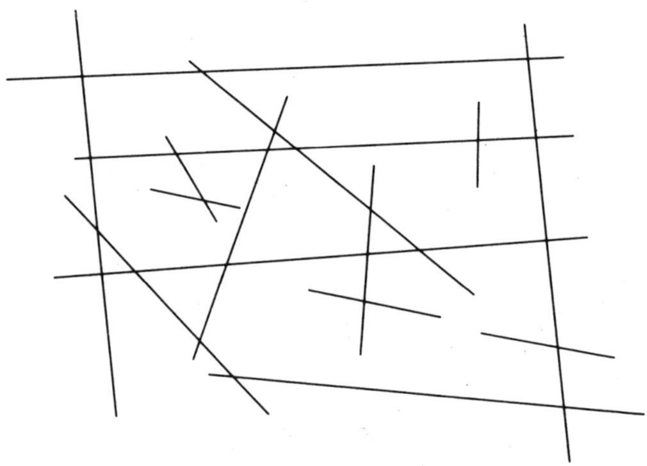

2 Which two numbers, one in the top circle and one in the bottom circle, are the odd ones out?

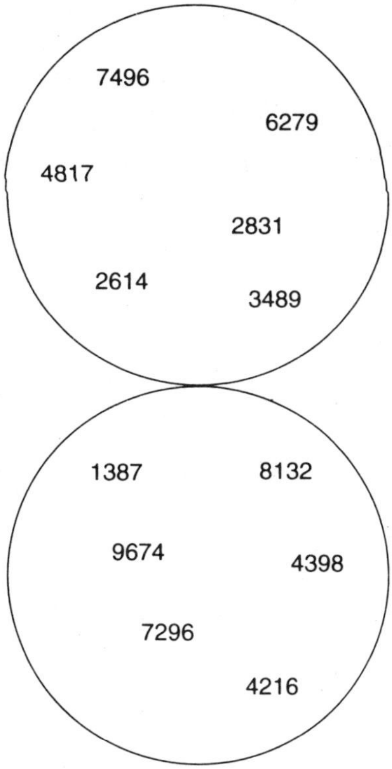

3 What number should replace the question mark?

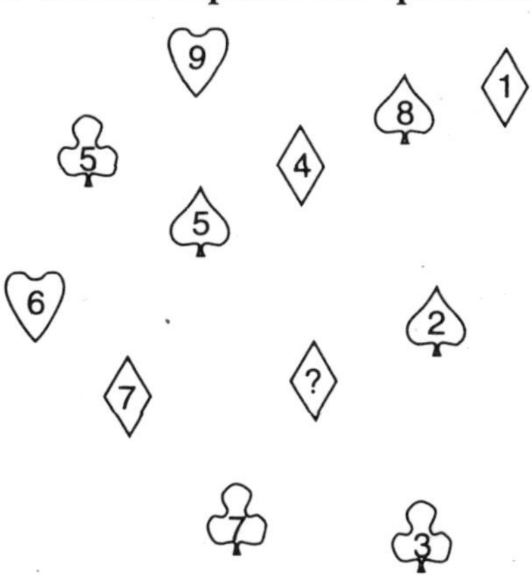

4 Which is the odd one out?

MODE, FASHION, TREND, DRESS, VOGUE

5 A familiar phrase has been split up and jumbled into three-letter groups. Find the saying. For example, FIND THE QUOTE could be jumbled up into DTH, OTE, FIN, EQU.

ATO, OTT, LIK, NAH, OOF, EAC, INR

6 ARC, AIL, ARM, SOB, AIR

What word below continues the above sequence?

CAT, ASS, COB, PIG, DOG

7 Using the letters in each square, together with the letter in the triangle, find four words which are all synonyms.

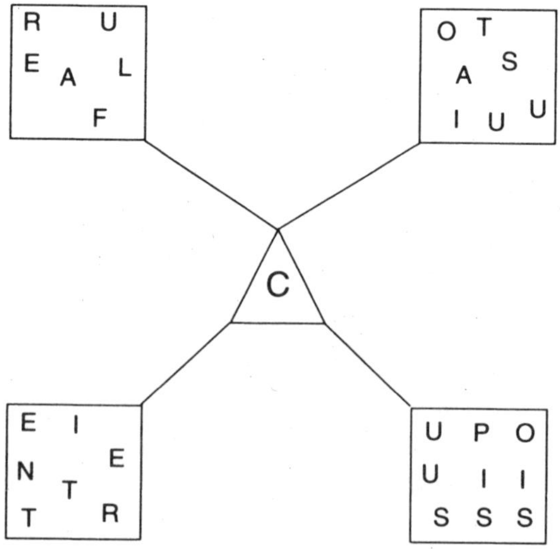

8 What is FAVEOLATE?

a) HONEYCOMBED
b) FRUITFUL
c) LEAF SHAPED
d) ORNATE JEWELLERY
e) THIN MORTAR

9

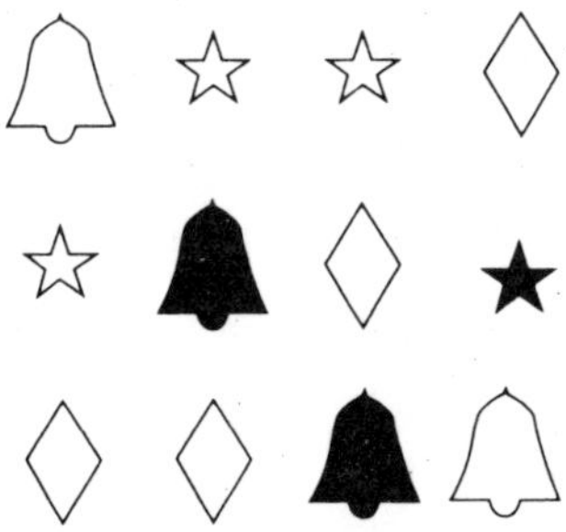

What comes next in the above sequence?

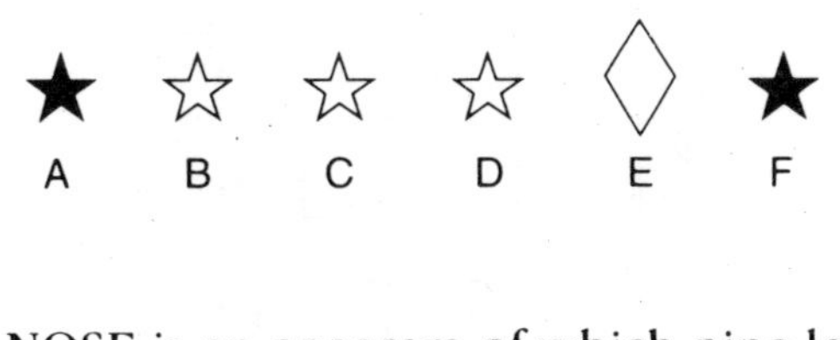

10 DUMPY NOSE is an anagram of which nine-letter word?

11 If presented with the words MAR, AM and FAR and asked to find the shortest word that contained all the letters from which these words could be produced you should come up with the word FARM.
Here is a further list of words:

PATROL PULSATE SCRUPLE

What is the shortest English word from which all these words can be produced?

12 JANUARY
FEBRUARY
APRIL
JULY
NOVEMBER
APRIL
OCTOBER
?

Which month comes next?

13 What numbers should replace the question marks?

1	3	4	2	6	1	3
2	4	3	1	6	2	4
6	1	3	4	2	6	1
4	3	1	?	?	4	3
2	6	1	?	?	2	6
3	1	6	2	4	3	1
4	2	6	1	3	4	2

14 ESTRANGE is to ALIENATE as PARTITION is to:

a) DECOLLATE
b) DETACH
c) FRAGMENT
d) PRESCIND
e) QUARANTINE

15 What number should replace the question mark?

7	
22	18
67	40
202	?
607	172

16

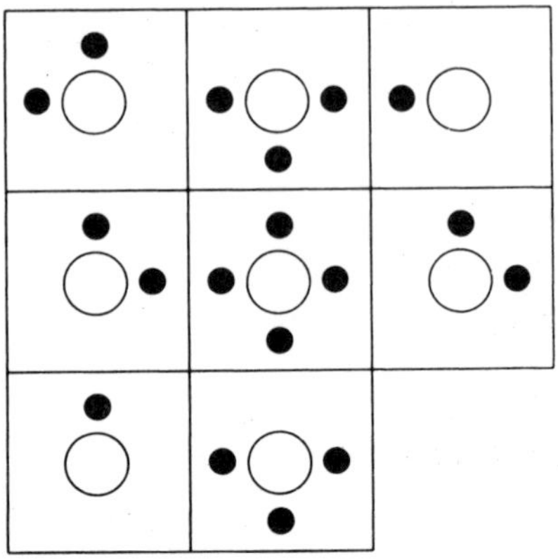

Which is the missing tile?

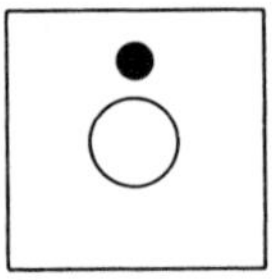

A

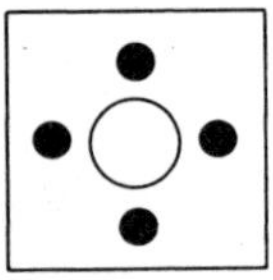

B

C

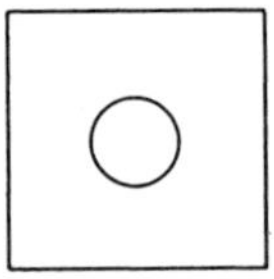

D

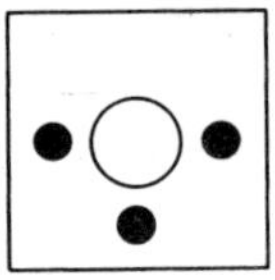

E

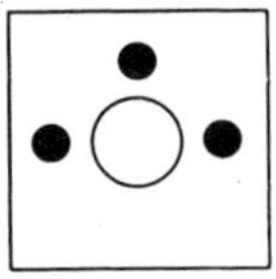

F

17 Which word in brackets is closest in meaning to the word in capitals?

INCARNATION (chant, indication, avatar, restriction, diabolism)

18 Reading clockwise, pick one letter from each circle in turn to spell out two antonyms. All letters are used and each word starts at a different circle.

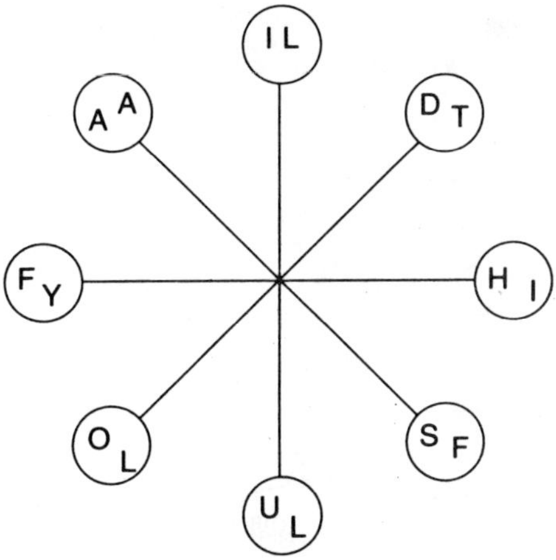

19 Insert a word that means the same as the definitions outside the brackets.

a light two-wheeled vehicle (   ) withdrawn or moody

20 Which is the odd one out?

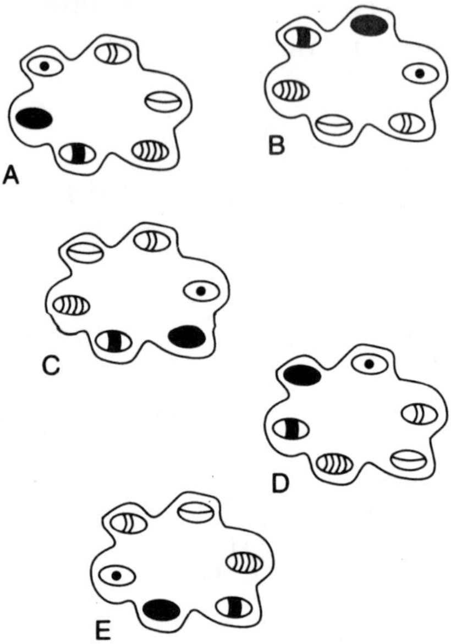

21 Which two words mean the same?

OBLIGATORY, INVIOLABLE, DIFFIDENT, CRITICAL, SQUEAMISH, SACROSANCT

22 Using only these five letters make a seven-letter word.

S E
R
A T

23 Which of these is not a medical term?

a) LLEGUT
b) RAXLYN
c) BIFLUA
d) GHIDNY
e) NIKYED

24 Find a word which when placed after these words makes new words?

MAN
DOT
LEVER (. . .)
DAM
COIN

25 What number should replace the question mark?

6	4	3	21
8	8	2	62
7	3	10	11
8	3	5	19
7	5	2	?

26 Fill in the blanks to find two words which are antonyms. You may move clockwise or anticlockwise.

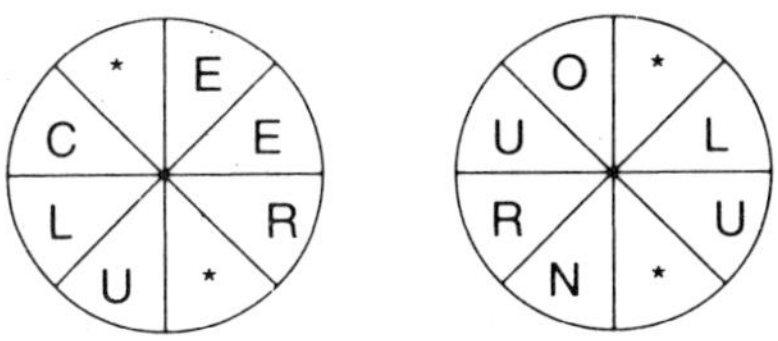

27 Each of the nine squares in the grid marked 1A to 3C should incorporate all the lines and symbols which are shown in the squares of the same letter and number immediately above and to the left. For example, 2B should incorporate all the lines and symbols that are in 2 and B.

One of the squares is incorrect. Which one is it?

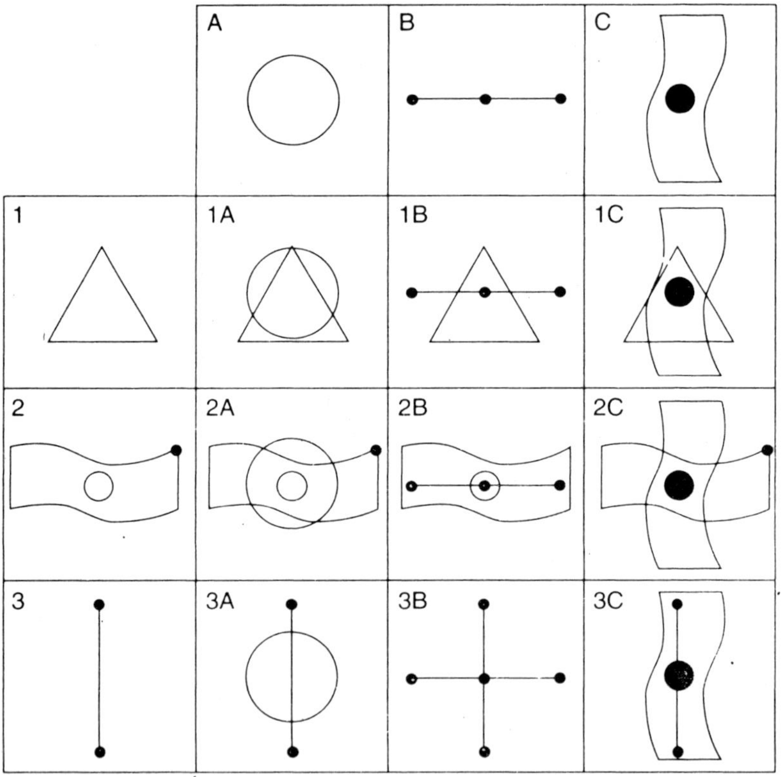

28 If 55 = 50

Then 44 = ?

29 HERD is to GIRAFFES as EXALTATION is to:

a) BEES
b) DUCKS
c) LARKS
d) POCHARD
e) PIGEONS

30 Which word means the same as FAIN?

a) EAGER
b) ASTUTE
c) INSIDIOUS
d) DEPLORE
e) DISTRESSED

31 The vowels have been omitted from this trite saying. See if you can replace them.

THDMM RTHLG HTTHG RTRTH SCNDL

32 Find a twelve-letter word by starting at a corner and moving towards the centre in a spiral.

P	H	I
O	C	L
M	A	I
E	A	H

33 Find a ten-letter word by moving from circle to circle. Each letter should be only used once.

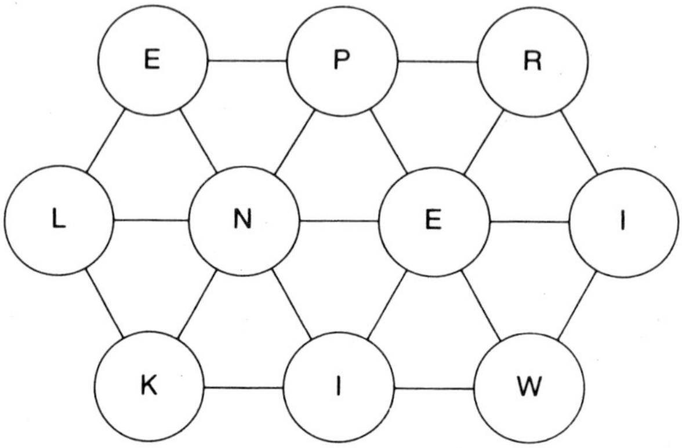

34 Complete the route.

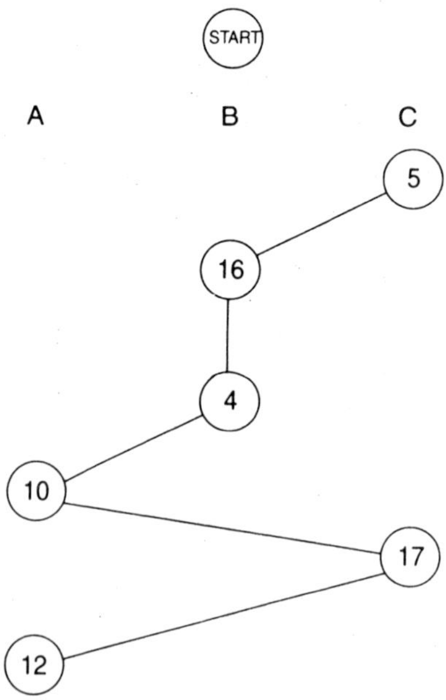

Where should 25 go – A, B, or C?

A B C

35 Simplify

$$\frac{2286}{4191}$$

36 Place two 3-letter bits together to make a fish.

HER OCT ICE UTE TRO PLA PUS RIN

37 Which two words mean the opposite?

INEXPLICABLE, HAZARDOUS, INSENSIBLE, CONSIDERATE, INSATIABLE, UNCERTAIN

38 What is GYNEPHOBIA the fear of?

a) RIDICULE
b) PAIN
c) WOMEN
d) STRANGERS
e) POVERTY

39 What letter should replace the question mark?

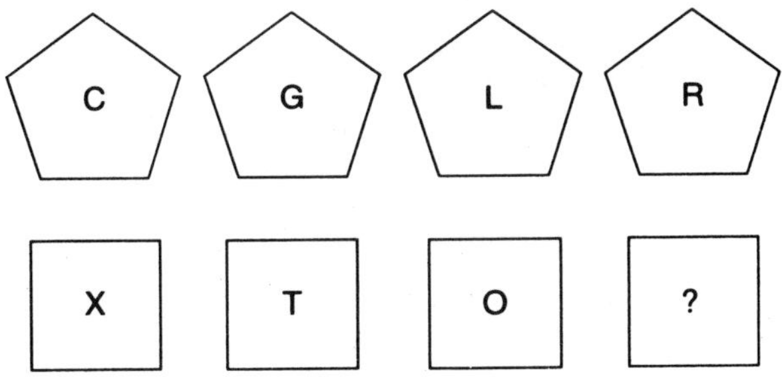

40 Solve the nine-letter word by finding the correct three-letter words.

E	S	I	A	S	R	A	E	A
B	P	N	D	K	O	G	G	N
*	*	*	*	*	*	*	*	*

Test six

1 What is the longest word that can be produced from the following ten letters?

BRIAONTCLF

2 Find the starting point and move from letter to adjacent letter horizontally and vertically, but not diagonally, to find a twelve-letter word. You must provide the missing letters.

A	*	T	A
L	O	I	*
O	C	*	U

3 A familiar phrase has been split up and jumbled into three letter groups. Find the saying. For example, FIND THE QUOTE could be jumbled up into DTH, OTE, FIN, *EQU*.

STA, EOF, STR, NCE, LIN, ESI, LEA

4 Which is the odd one out?

VOCIFERATE, ARGUE, YELL, RANT, RAVE

5

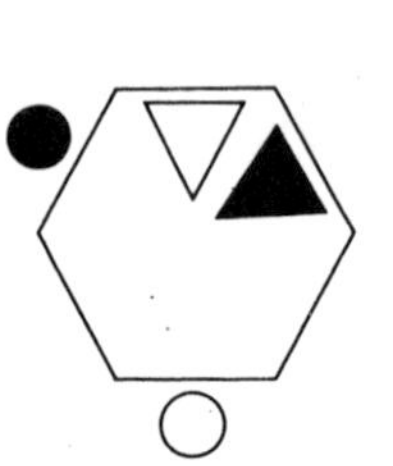

is to

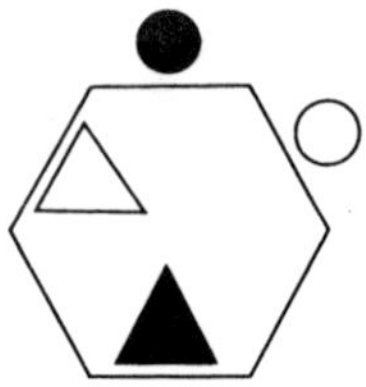

as

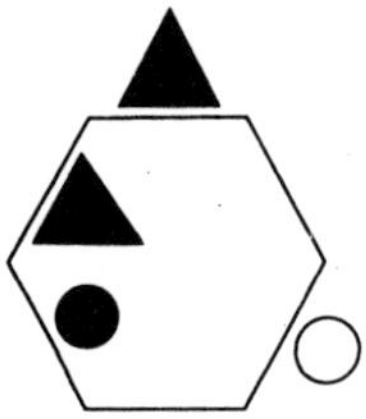

is to

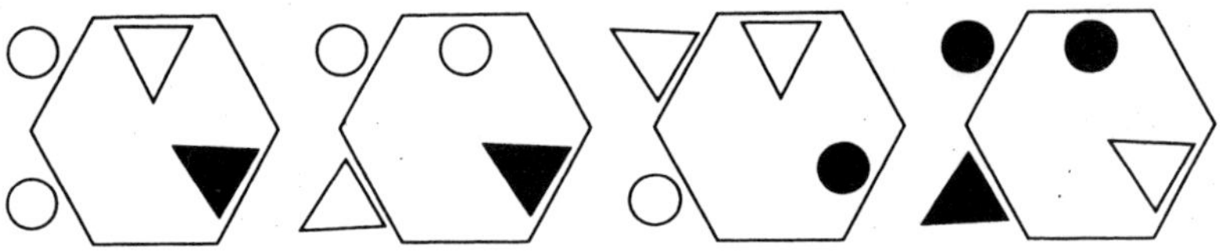

A B C D

6 **What number should replace the question mark?**

2	7	5	6	8	3	2	1
4	9	3	7	1	5	7	2
7	6	9	3	9	8	9	3
1	8	4	7	6	2	3	8
?	5	4	1	6	1	3	1

7 **BRUTISH DEBTOR is an anagram of which two words, which are synonyms (7,6)?**

8 What number should replace the question mark?

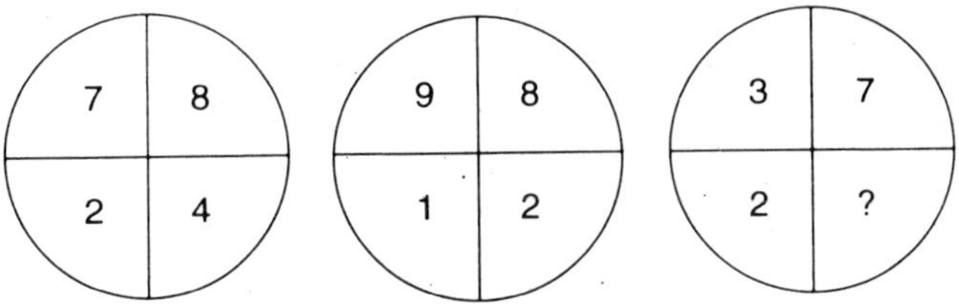

9

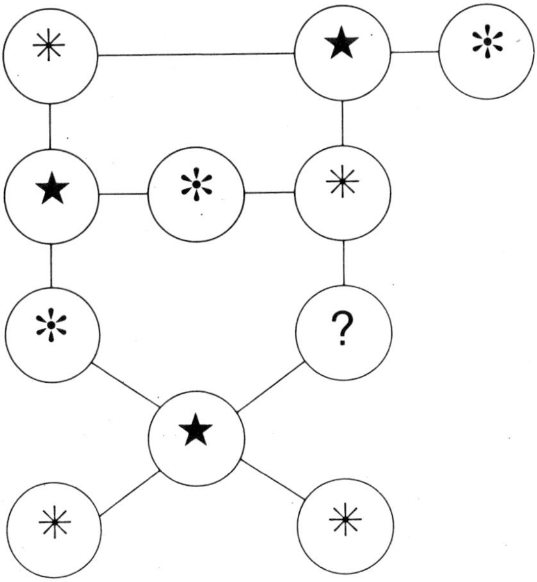

What should replace the question mark?

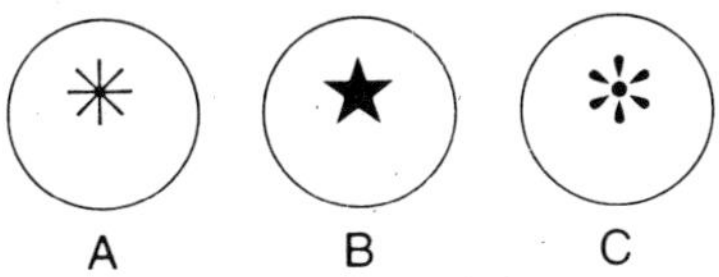

10 To what does the adjective LITTORAL refer?

a) the church
b) the countryside
c) the shore
d) a work of literature
e) speech

11 Spiral clockwise to find a ten-letter word. Only alternate letters are shown.

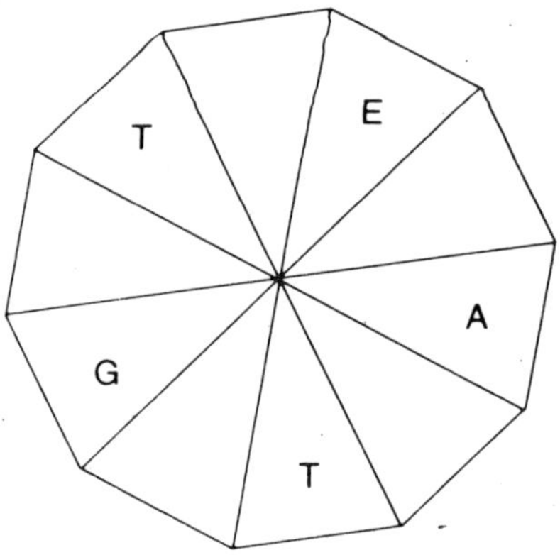

12 Which number is the odd one out?

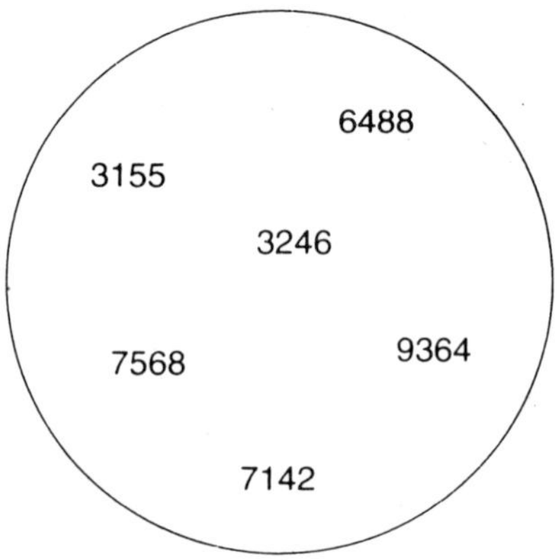

13 Which word in brackets is closest in meaning to the word in capitals?

EXULT (obtain, jubilate, appreciate, liberate, facilitate)

14 Complete the numbers in the final column.

2	7	6	?
1	4	4	?
9	7	5	?
8	2	6	?

15 Which is the odd one out?

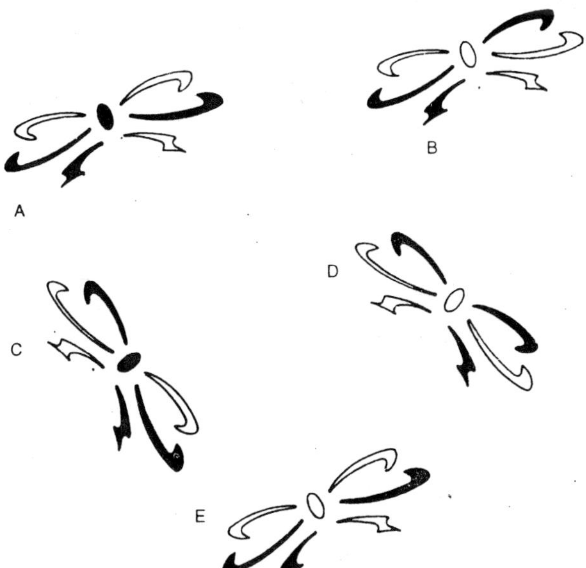

16 Insert two letters into each bracket so that they finish the words on the left and start the words on the right. The letters inserted should spell out a six-letter word when read downwards in pairs.

PI (**) CK
SH (**) IT
SO (**) AN

17 Which two words that sound alike but are spelled differently mean:

tiniest/let

18 Write down the figure for thirteen thousand, thirteen hundred and thirteen.

19 BALLYHOO is to COMMOTION as REVELRY is to:
a) CLAMOURING
b) ROISTERING
c) FURORE
d) RUCTION
e) RAZZMATAZZ

20

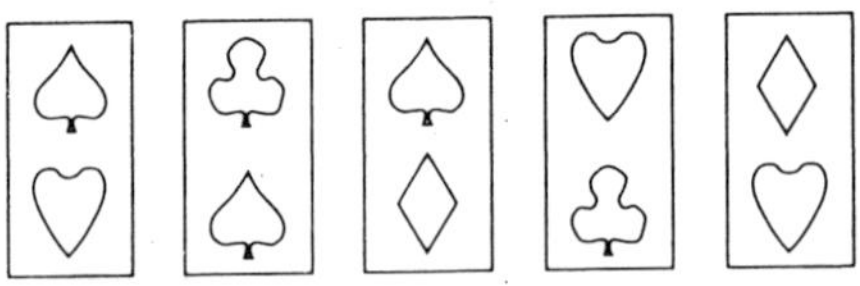

Which option below completes the above set?

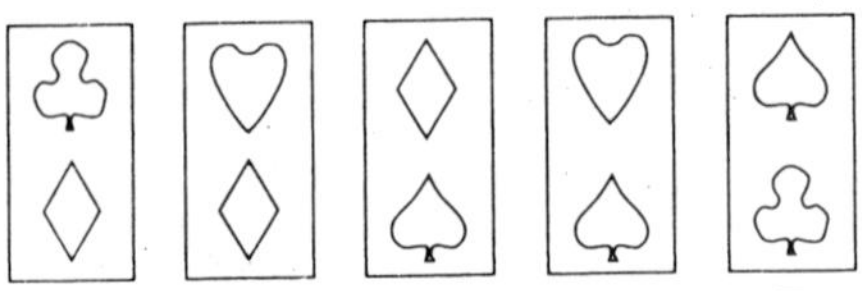

A B C D E

21 Find a ten-letter word which is a flower.

. E . I . T . O . E

22 Find three fish.

. O . B . A . L .
. W . R . F . S .
. R . M . E . E .

23 Place two three-letter bits together to make an animal.

TIG SEL BEA CAT PON
TLI WEA IER VED IED

24 Find a ten-letter word which is a tree.

U . A . Y . T . S

25 Place eight pairs of letters together to make two 8-letter words. One pair is not used.

BI	BA	IN
LA	SU	NT
CU	TE	JU

26 Fill in the blanks to find two words which are antonyms. You may move either clockwise or anticlockwise.

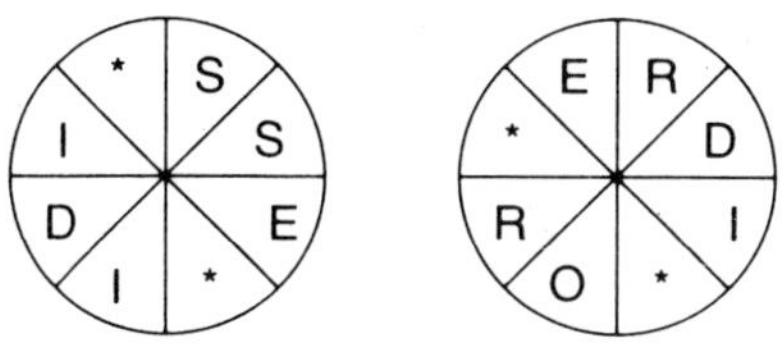

27

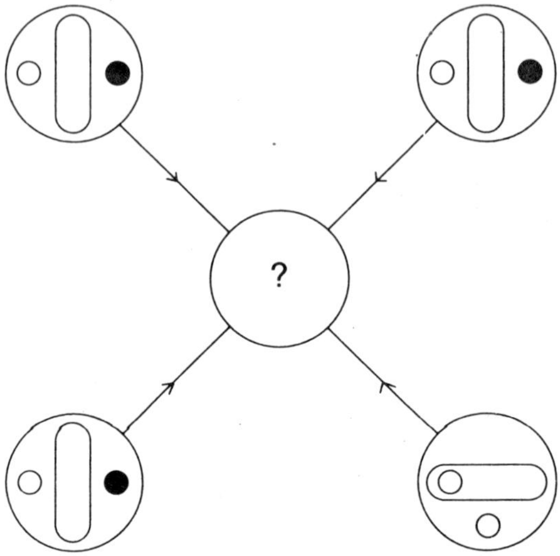

Each line and symbol which appears in the four outer circles above is transferred to the centre circle according to these rules:

If a line or symbol occurs in the outer circles:

Once: it is transferred
Twice: it is possibly transferred
Three times: it is transferred
Four times: it is not transferred

Which of the circles shown below should appear at the centre of the diagram, above?

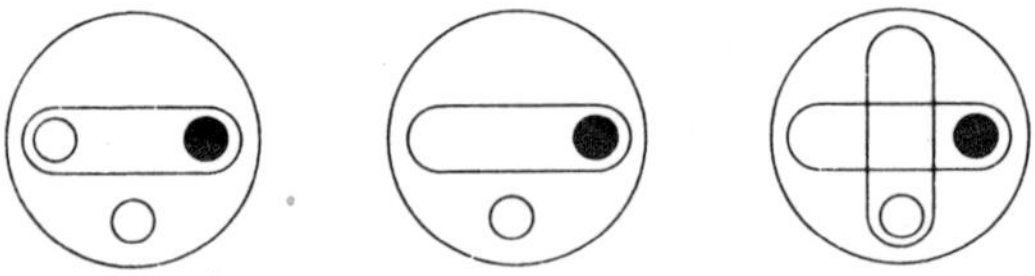

A B C

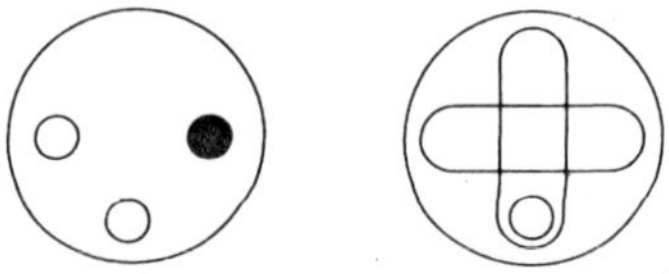

D E

28 What is the name given to a group of mallard?

a) SORD
b) SKEIN
c) STALK
d) SPRING

29 Which word means the opposite of UPSET?

a) APPEASEMENT
b) TURPITUDE
c) DEGRADED
d) PENSIVE
e) RECTIFICATION

30 Find a six-letter word made up of only these four letters.

P E
T S

31 What number should replace the question mark?

6.72, 6.10, 6.66, 6.16, 6.60, 6.22, 6.54, ?

32 This nine-letter word has been mixed up. See if you can unravel it.

E	I	S
P	O	C
N	V	R

33 After the letters are rearranged, three of the circles will contain a six-letter word, one will not. Which one?

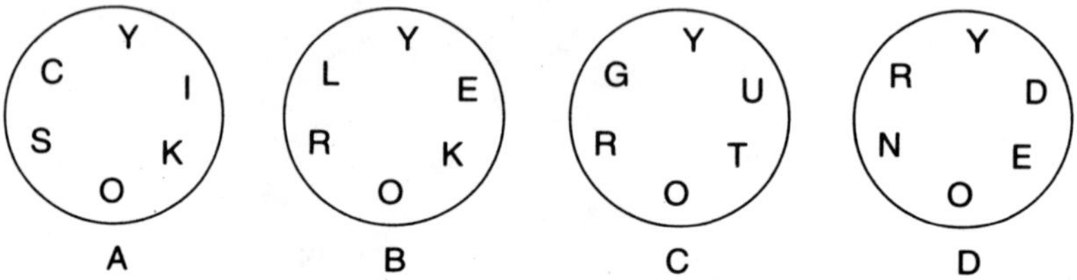

34 Find a ten-letter word by travelling along the lines.

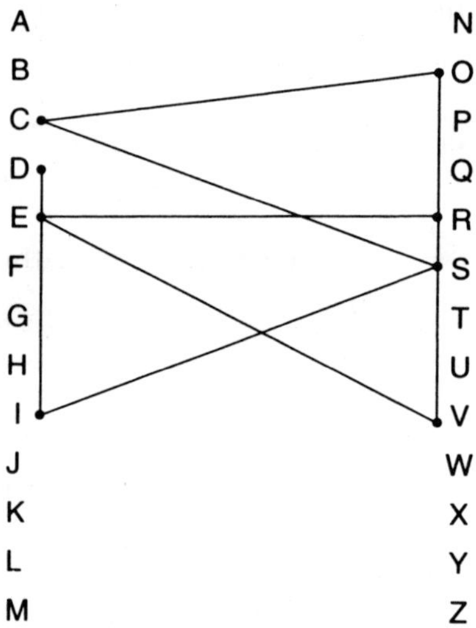

35 Change $\frac{17}{18}$ to a decimal.

36 Simplify

$$\frac{1890}{2940}$$

37 Place two 4-letter bits together to equal a drink.

SCHN	NTHE	COCK	POUC
BURG	ADER	APES	MUSC
HONC	ABSI	TIAL	UNDI

38 Which two words mean the same?

IMBROGLIO, HIDDEN, ENVIOUS, INVENTIVE, MODISH, SCORN, COMPLEXITY

39 Which word when placed in front of these words makes apt phrases?

CAKE
BAG
(. . . . . .) BATH
DOWN
FINGER

40 This nine-letter word has been mixed up. See if you can unravel it.

N	E	I
O	S	I
T	R	R

Test seven

1

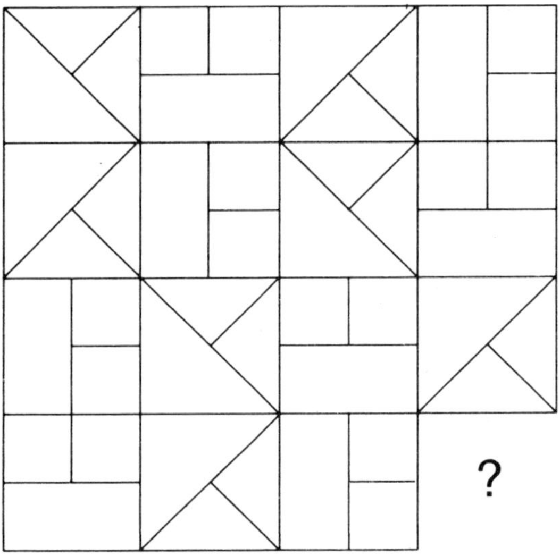

Which square should replace the question mark?

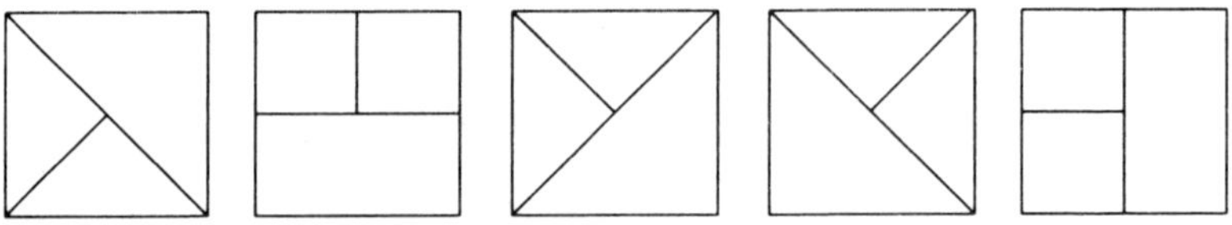

A B C D E

2 What number should replace the question mark?

3	8	4	3	1	2	8
8	7	6	4	2	1	9
7	8	4	?	1	1	2

3 FLAUNTER PERIL is an anagram of which two words that are opposite in meaning (4, 9)?

4 Find the starting point and spiral clockwise round the perimeter to spell out a nine-letter word, finishing at the central letter. You have to provide the missing letters.

I	E	*
R	E	A
*	*	N

5 How many minutes is it before 12 noon if 42 minutes ago it was five times as many minutes past 9 a.m.?

6 Which word in brackets is most nearly opposite to the word in capitals?

SEDENTARY (temporal, torpid, loyal, mobile, uncertain)

7 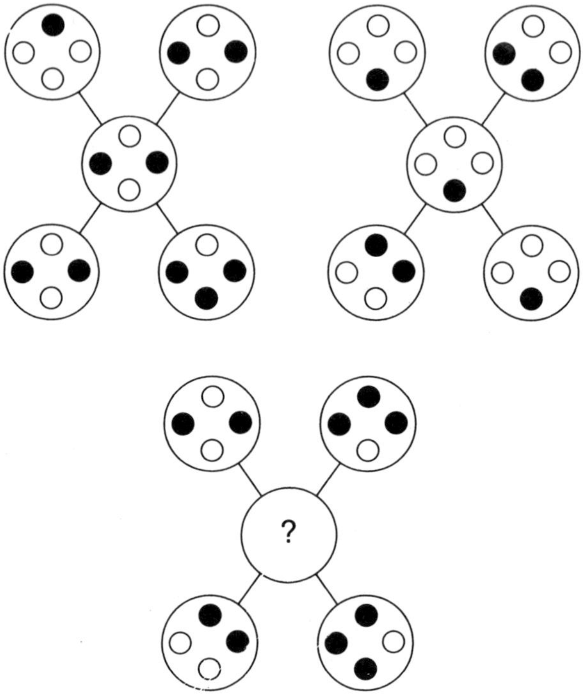

Which circle should replace the one with the question mark?

A B C D E

8 Read clockwise to find two words, one in each circle, that are antonyms. You must provide the missing letters.

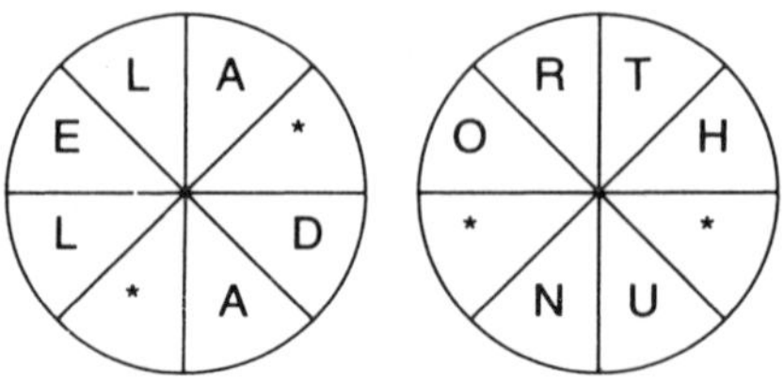

9 Solve the cryptic clue below (13 letters). The answer is an anagram contained within the clue.

Reassurance for one cute German in disarray

10 What letters should replace the question mark?

G	R	?
E	P	?
H	S	W
F	Q	?

11 What number should replace the question mark?

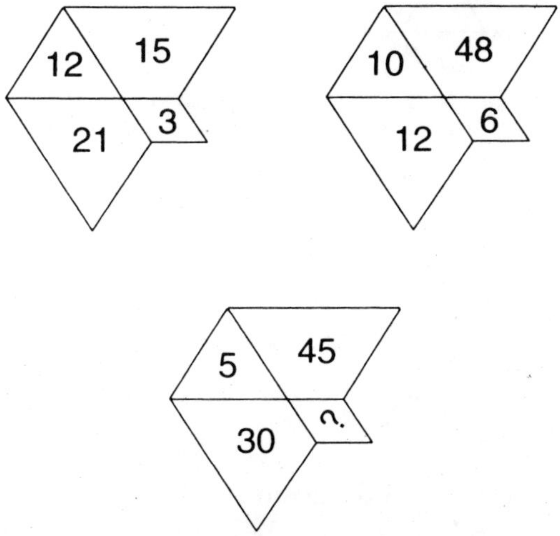

12 Which two words that are anagrams of each other solve the following clues?

concealed faculty

13 What do the following have in common?

TAXI RANK
GLOSS PAINT
TOM AND JERRY

14 Which is the odd one out?

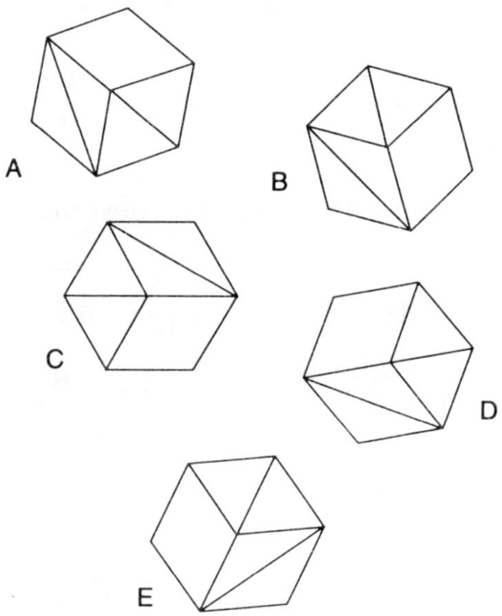

15 LAIR (CAROLINE) ONCE

What girl's name should go in the brackets below according to the same rules as in the example above?

RAIN (. . . . .) NEED

16 What number should replace the question mark?

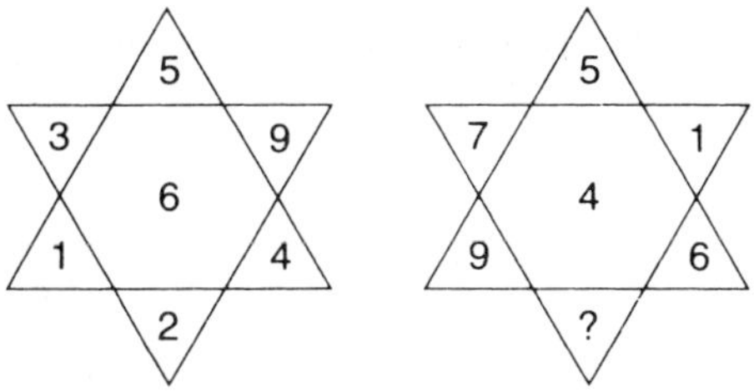

17 Insert the name of a type of tree into the bottom row to complete the eight three-letter words reading downwards.

H	F	P	T	S	M	B	M
I	L	A	A	E	A	A	A
*	*	*	*	*	*	*	*

18 Which word is the odd one out?

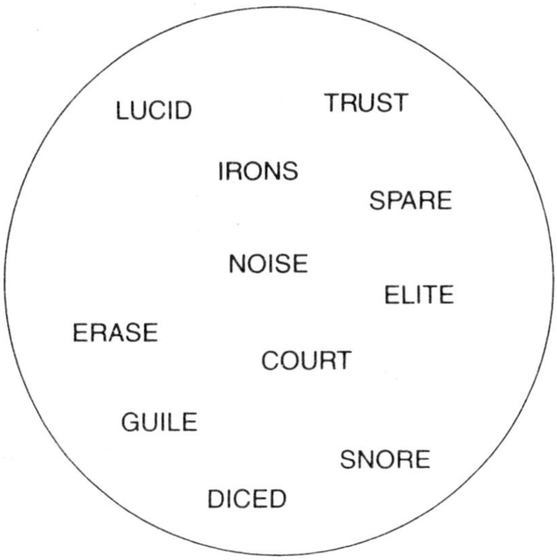

19 PALLET is to GOODS as PODIUM is to:

SCAFFOLD, CANDIDATE, CONDUCTOR, PERFORMER, PLATFORM

20 Which is the odd one out?

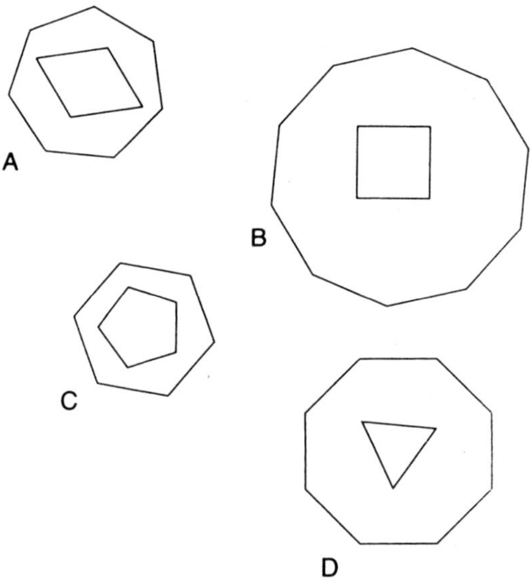

21 If

F = 3
Z = 2
K = 4
B = 0

what does C represent?

22 Find a seven-letter word using only these five letters.

N		L
	I	
O		P

23 What is CHIONOPHOBIA the fear of?

a) RUIN
b) WORDS
c) SNOW
d) WATER
e) THUNDER

24 Find this ten-letter name for a sporting arena.

. I . P . D . O . E

25 What number should replace the question mark?

20	8	2	24
17	9	3	24
16	7	4	36
9	6	5	15
8	3	6	?

26 Find a ten-letter word by moving from circle to circle. Each letter must only be used once.

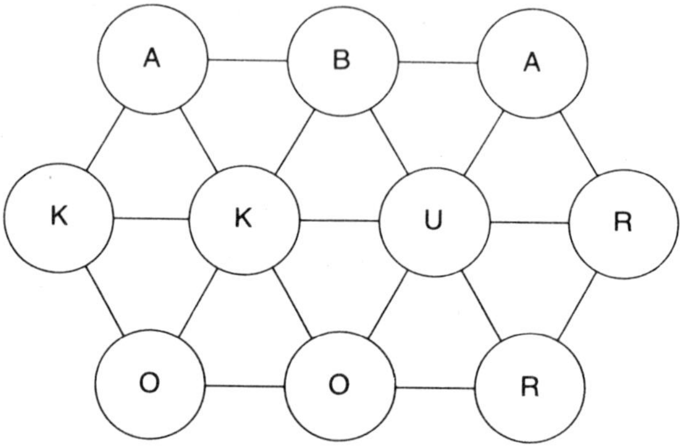

27 Each of the nine squares in the grid marked 1A to 3C should incorporate all the lines and symbols which are shown in the squares of the same letter and number immediately above and to the left. For example, 2B should incorporate all the lines and symbols that are in 2 and B.

One of the squares is incorrect. Which one is it?

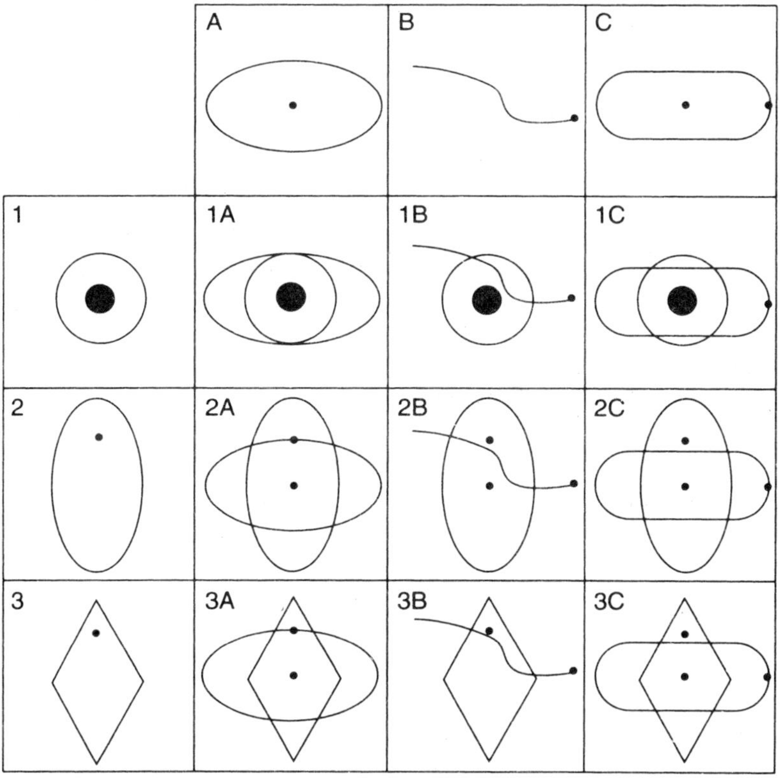

28 All the vowels have been omitted from this trite saying. See if you can replace them.

FSMNS YSMXP NSVTH YWLLB

29 Place two 3-letter bits together to make a fruit.

CHE	SON	BAN	PEA	PEC
RED	CHI	RRI	DAM	ANI

30 Which anagram is not a coin?

a) CUDSOE
b) KINLEC
c) BULEOR
d) KESHEL
e) ROWHAR

31 Which two words mean the same?

FLORID, TRANSLUCENT, LUCID, LIMITED, BALEFUL, FLUSHED, DECEITFUL

32 Find a twelve-letter word by starting at a corner and moving to the centre in a spiral.

A	N	A
I	S	E
T	T	S
E	H	T

33 Fill in the blanks to find two words which are antonyms. You may move clockwise or anticlockwise.

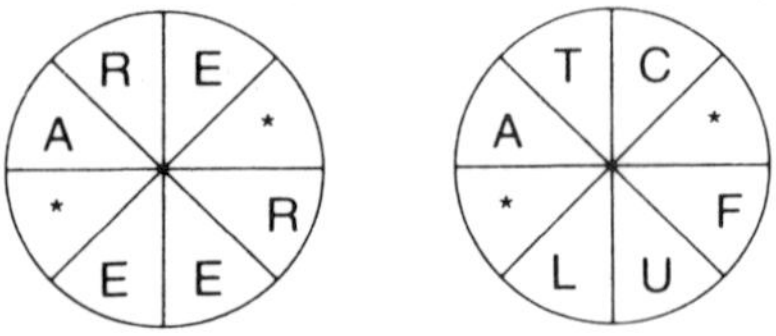

34 How many squares plus rectangles are there in this diagram?

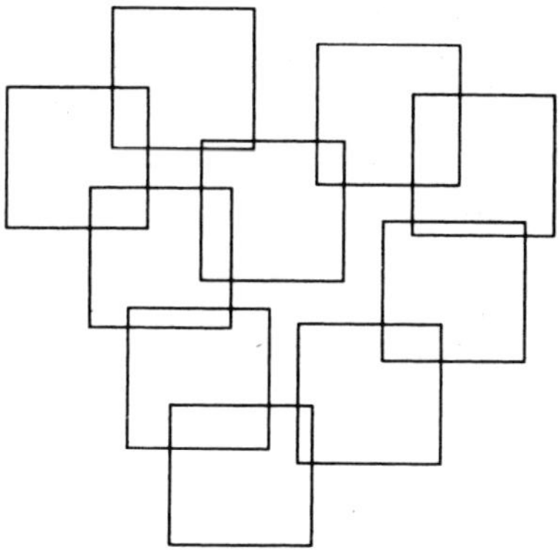

35 Simplify

$6 - 7 \times 3 + 8 \div 2 =$

36 Find a one-word anagram of

VOICES RANT ON

There is a clue in the puzzle.

37 HORDE is to SAVAGES as MURDER is to:

a) SWANS
b) WRENS
c) CURLEWS
d) CROWS

38 What is always part of PICOT?

a) an embroidered shirt
b) a loop
c) a type of aeroplane
d) a newsletter
e) a pipe of peace

39 What does this mathematical sign mean?

$\pm$

a) plus or minus
b) divided by
c) not equal to
d) not divided by
e) ratio

40 Which is the odd one out?

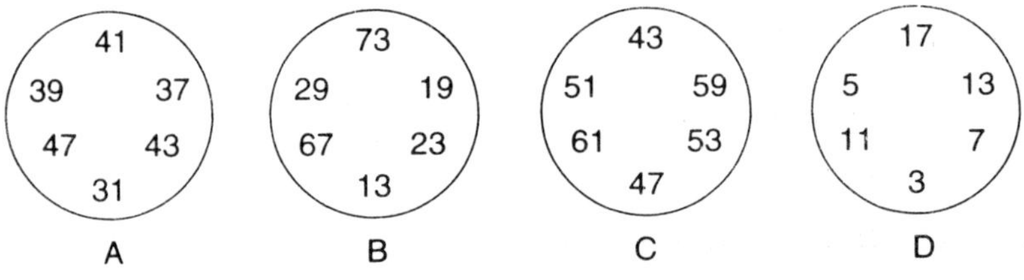

Test eight

1

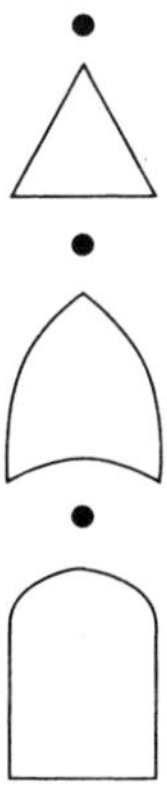

is to

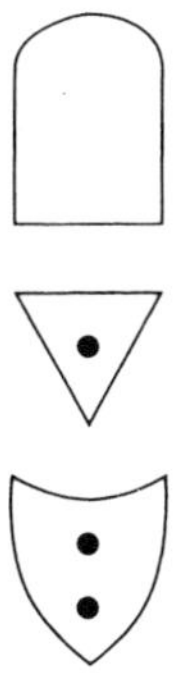

as

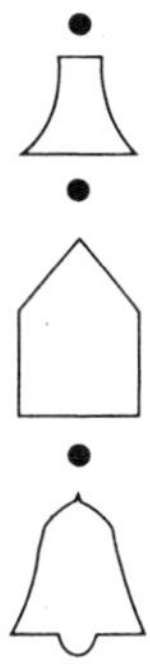

is to

A

B

C

D

E

F

2 My watch showed the correct time at 12 noon, but then the battery started to run down until it eventually stopped completely. Between 12 noon and when it stopped, it lost 20 minutes per hour on average. It now shows 6 p.m., but it stopped 4 hours ago. What is the correct time now?

3 Which is the odd one out?

RAVEN, EBONY, CARMINE, SABLE, JET

4 DISPUTES GALES is an anagram of which two words that have opposite meanings (6, 7)?

5 ALK = 8
SNT = 5
MOE = 8
TIC = ?

6 CAT, FERAL, SARDINE, PROACTIVE

What comes next in the above sequence?

SIMULTANEOUS, SUBORDINATE, NEGOTIATION, INOCULATED, LEGISLATURE

7 Out of 100 people surveyed, 87 had an egg for breakfast, 79 had toasted bread, 68 had bacon and 96 had coffee. How many people, at least, must have had all four items, i.e. egg, bacon, toast and coffee?

8

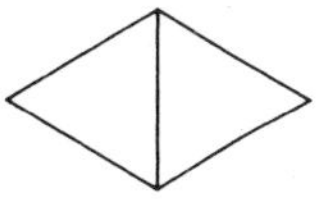

is to

as

is to

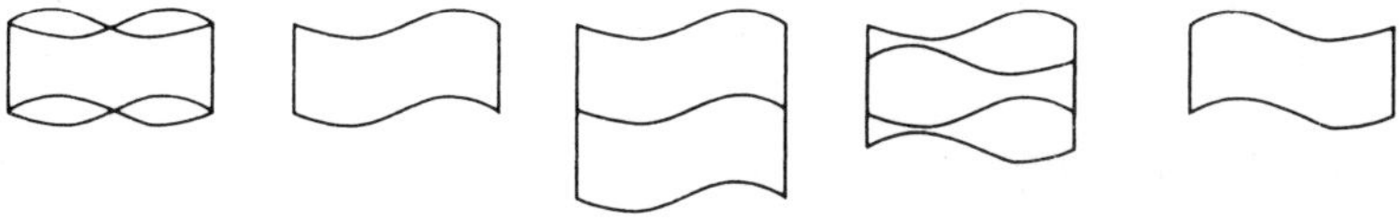

A B C D E

9 Which of the following is not an anagram of a type of sport?

all babes
hear cry
a taker
a krona
lose cars

10 What letter is missing from the wall?

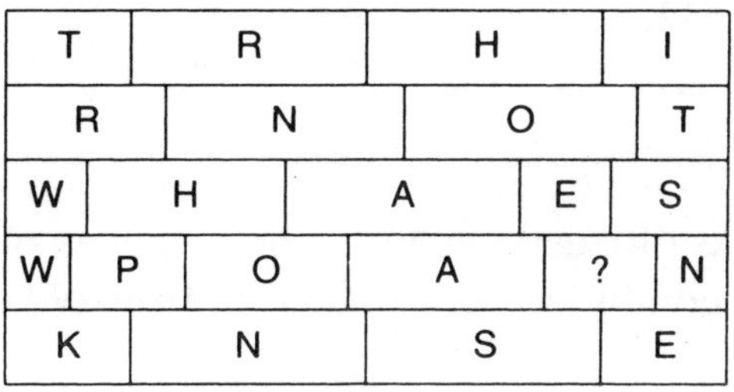

11 Arrange the three-letter bits into the correct order to construct an amusing sentence.

DON, AWS, IFM, INL, EWE, LYO,

ARR, UTL, AWS, IAG, REO,

AVE, LDH, UTL, AWE, WOU

12 Use each letter of the newspaper headline below once each to spell out three types of bird.

MEET PORKY GUINEA-PIG!

13 784326 is to 286734 as 913452 is to ?

14 ORB is to RUE as PRY is to ?

15 Add three consecutive letters of the alphabet to the word below, without splitting the consecutive letters, to form another word.

SING

16 Insert the name of a kitchen utensil into the bottom line to complete the eight 3-letter words reading downwards.

H	P	Y	A	C	R	L	P
A	E	O	R	U	A	E	E
*	*	*	*	*	*	*	*

17 Alf is half as old again as Jim, who is half as old again as Sid. Their combined ages total 171. How old are the three men?

18 What number should replace the question mark?

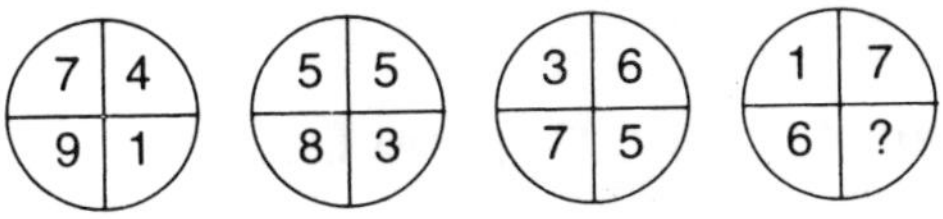

19

is to

as

is to

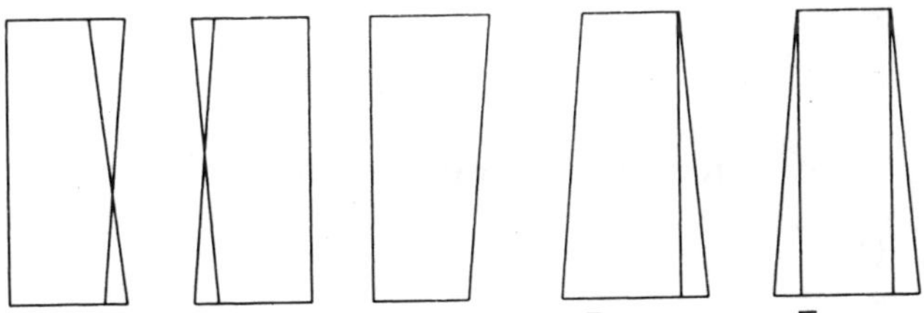

A B C D E

20 It is better to have a (____) (____) than to be (____).
Oscar Wilde

(____) is no (____) for a good (____)
Fran Lebowitz

The English (____) (____) any man who has no (____) and is (____) about it.
James Agate

Place the ten words below correctly to complete the three quotations.

personality, admire, modest, humility, fascinating, income, talent, substitute, instinctively, permanent

21 Find three birds.

. O . M . R . N .
. O . D . I . C .
. T . N . C . A .

22 Find a six-letter word using only these four letters.

W O
R S

23 Which word means the same as MODISH?

a) UNPLEASANT
b) COVETOUS
c) ASSIDUOUS
d) FASHIONABLE
e) VEXATIOUS

24 What is always part of a LANDAU?

a) EIGHT SEATS
b) TWO HORSES
c) A FOLDING TOP
d) AN ESCORT
e) SIX WHEELS

25 Which word when placed in front of these words makes new words?

FULLY
THRUSH
(. . . .) LIKE
BIRD
BOOK

26 This nine-letter word has been mixed up. See if you can unravel it.

P	A	L
R	S	E
L	I	C

27

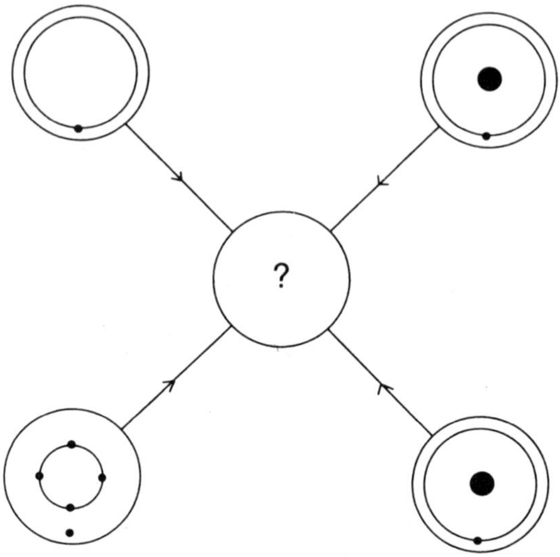

Each line and symbol which appears in the four outer circles, above is transferred to the centre circle according to these rules:

If a line or symbol occurs in the outer circles:

Once: it is transferred
Twice: it is possibly transferred
Three times: it is transferred
Four times: it is not transferred

Which of the circles shown below should appear at the centre of the diagram, above?

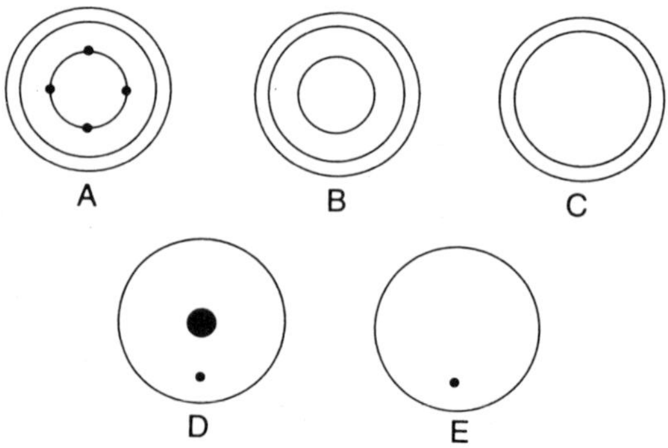

28 If 20 = 32 then 29 = ?

29 Place two three-letter bits together to make a tree.

BEE APP LED LOW
BED MAP WIL CHI

30 Which two words mean the opposite?

VORACIOUS, SADNESS, HELPMATE, ADVERSARY, ENORMITY, PELLUCID

31 Find this ten-letter word.

ANCIENT VEHICLE

. U . G . R . A . T

32 What does this mathematical sign mean

$\ngtr$

a) less than 10
b) greater than
c) identical with
d) not less than
e) not greater than

33 After the letters have been rearranged three of the circles will form a word, one will not. Which one?

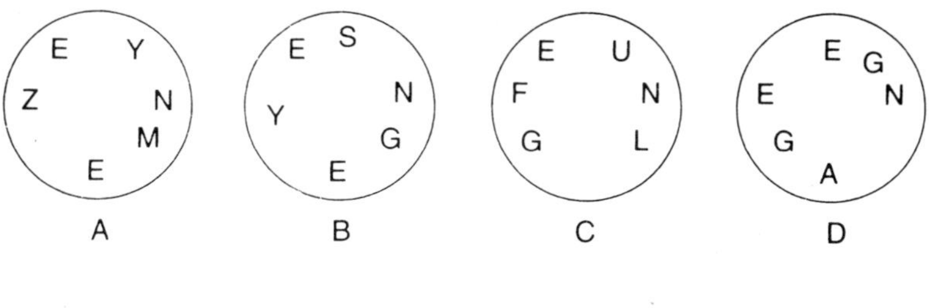

34 Find the order, to slide 1-2-3 into A-B-C so as to make three six-letter words.

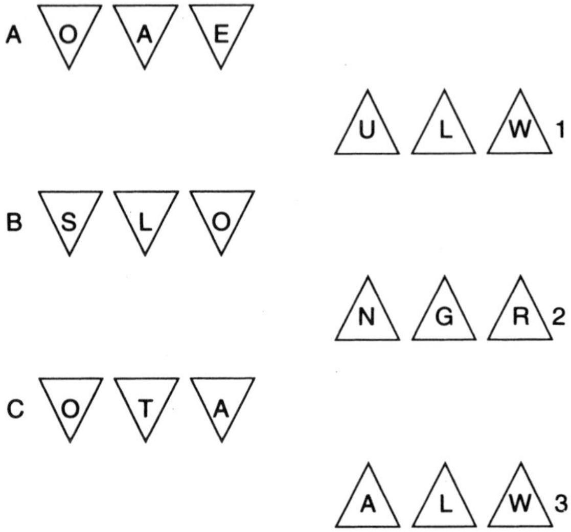

35 Simplify

$6 - 10 \times 2 - 12 \times 4$

36 What is the name given to a group of owls?

a) PITYING
b) PACK
c) PARK
d) PARLIAMENT

37 Find a ten-letter word which is a naval term.

. I . S . I . M . N

38 What is a MOUNTEBANK?

a) an animal
b) a charlatan
c) a mounted soldier
d) a river wall
e) a magistrate

39 Which circle is the odd one out?

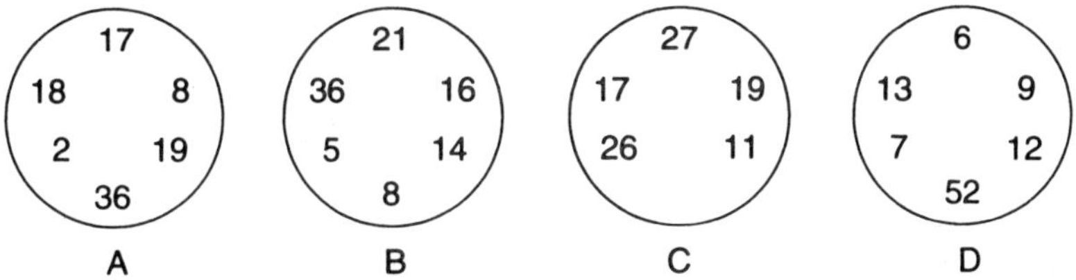

40 Fill in the blanks to find an eight-letter word which is a bird. You may move either clockwise or anticlockwise.

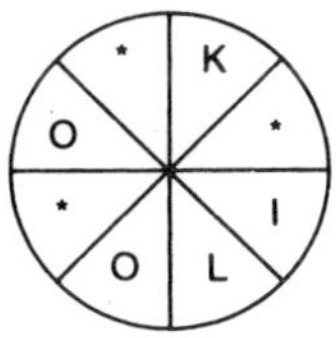

Test nine

1

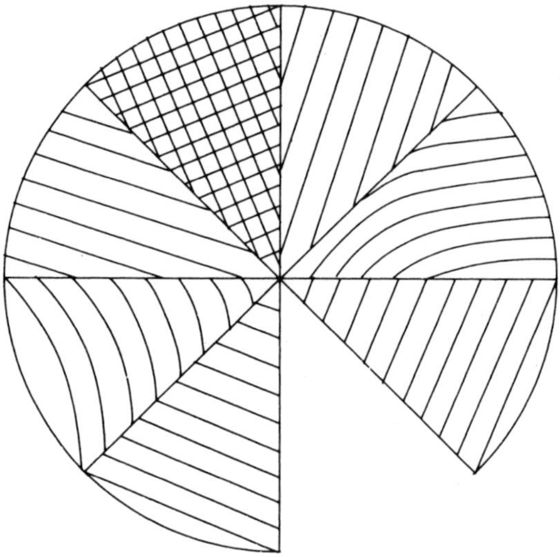

Which is the missing section

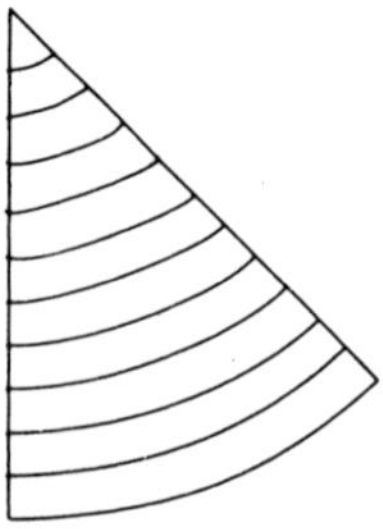

A

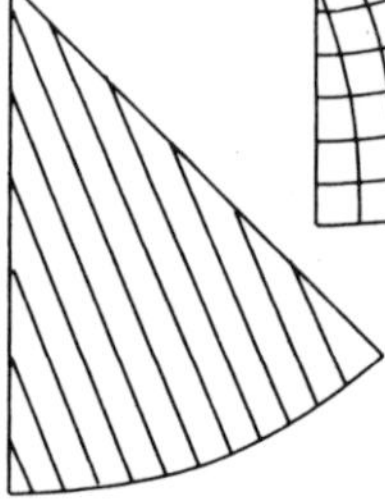

B

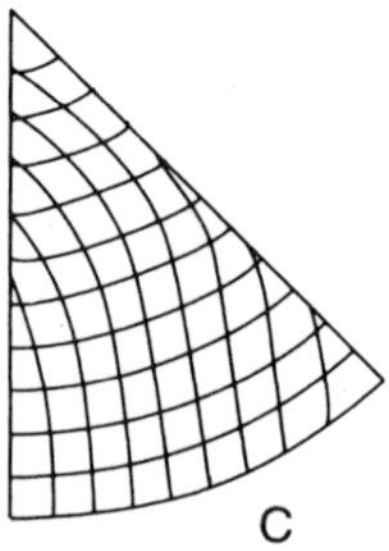

C

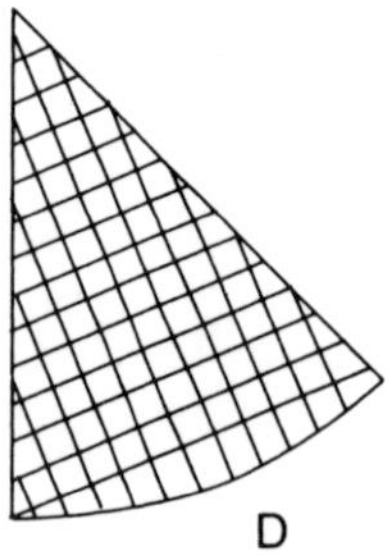

D

2 Divide 56 by a quarter and add 7. How many have you got?

3 FEARED YELLOW BOG is an anagram of which two words that mean the same (7, 8)?

4 Change one letter only in each word to produce a familiar phrase.

HEAL SO READ

5 Insert a word that means the same as the definitions outside the brackets.

grasp (   ) a brood of chickens

6 Which is the odd one out?

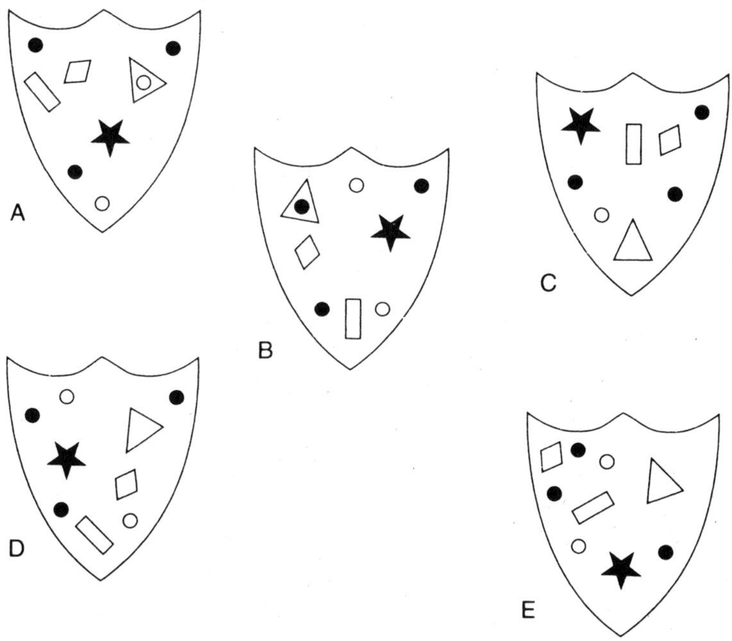

7 Only one set of letters below can be arranged into a five-letter word. Can you find the word?

YRABU
PENTH
CROLE
LUDGE
MCEAP
TUCVO

8 Which three letters should replace the question marks?

					C					
				L		K				
			?		?		?			
		K		C		M		L		
	L		M		C		K		L	
C		M		L		K		C		M

9 Frasier and Daphne share a box of chocolates in the ratio of 4 : 7. If Daphne has 28 chocolates, how many has Frasier?

10 Solve the cryptic clue below (13 letters). The answer is an anagram contained within the clue.

Play for time when writing satanic report

11 What does the following mnemonic enable you to do correctly?

Mnemonics neatly eliminate man's only nemesis – insufficient cerebral storage.

12 Complete the pyramid with seven words, one in each row, i.e. 1 × 1-letter, 1 × 2-letter, 1 × 3-letter etc. In each line a new letter is added anywhere, but without changing the order of the letters in the word above; for example A, AT, CAT, CART.

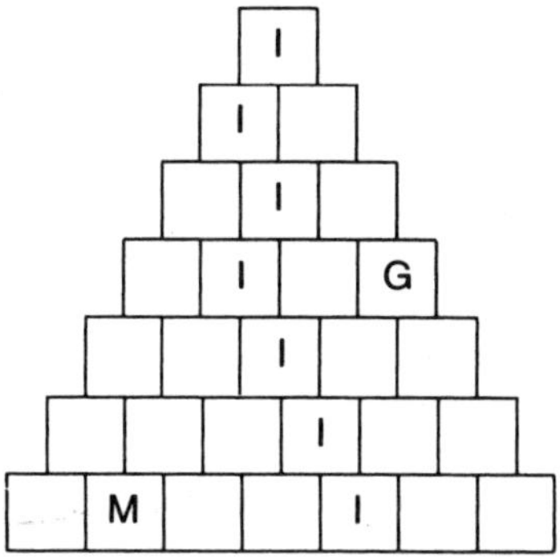

13 Which two words that are anagrams of each other solve the following clue.

DISTANT SHOOTING STAR

14 Which is the odd one out?

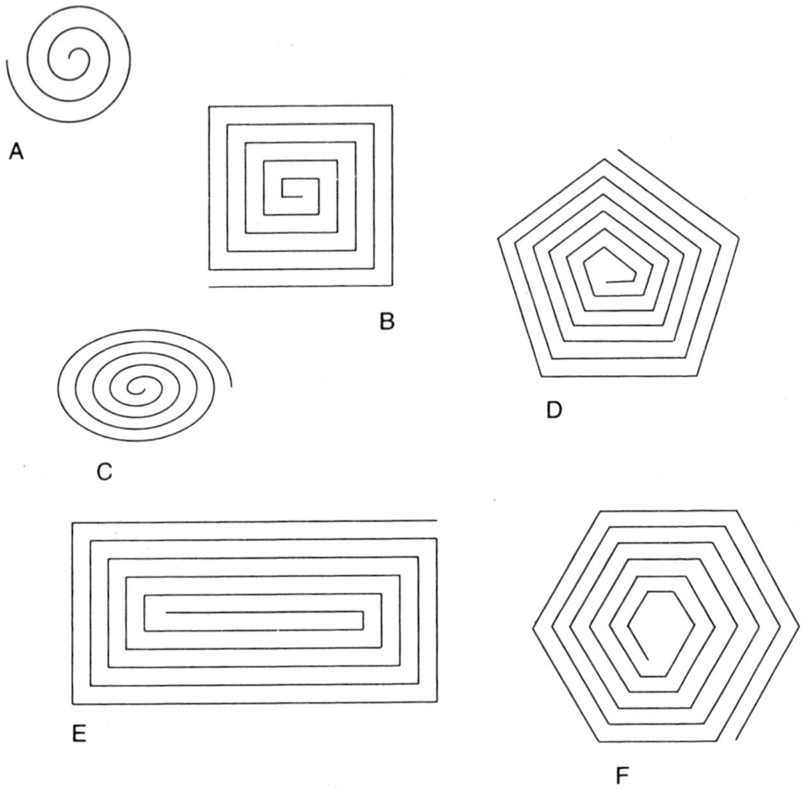

15 You have picked 437 tomatoes from your greenhouse, which you are putting in bags to give to your neighbours. You wish to put an equal number of tomatoes into each bag, and you wish to use as few bags as possible. How many tomatoes should you put into how many bags?

16 Where should the letter H appear in the grid?

A	B		C		
	E				D
			F		
		G			
I					

17 SIERRA is to MOUNTAIN as WADI is to:

a) RAVINE
b) LAKE
c) GRASSLAND
d) PLATEAU
e) HILL

18 Find the starting point and visit every square once only to reach the treasure marked T. 2E 1S means two squares east and one square south.

N

2E 2S	1W 1S	2S 2W
1E 1S	1N 1E	2W 1N
1N 2E	T	1W 2N

W (left side), E (right side)

S

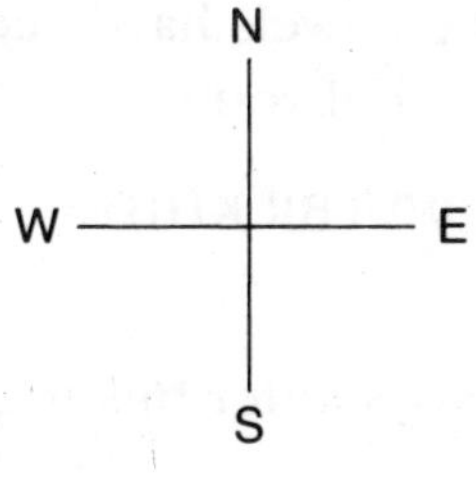

19 A man has 53 coloured socks in his drawer: 18 identical blue socks, 27 identical red socks and 8 identical brown socks. The lights have failed and he is left completely in the dark. How many socks must he take out of the drawer to be 100% certain that he then has at least one pair of each colour?

20

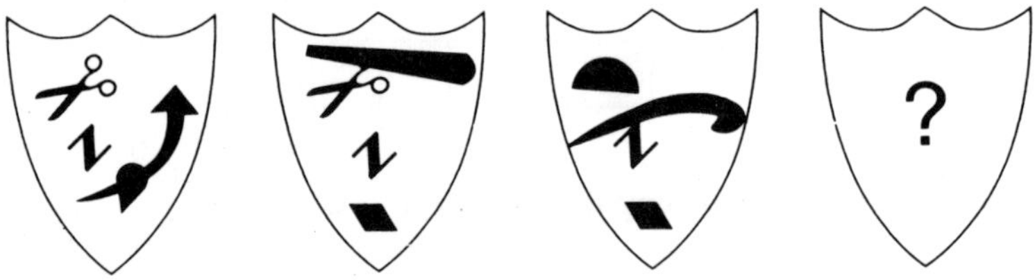

Which shield below continues the above sequence?

A B C D E

21 All of the vowels have been omitted from this trite saying. See if you can replace them.

THBST WYTBR KHBTS TDRPT

22 Place two 3-letter bits together to make a bird.

LED PEE CHO GON PLO VEN REE
WID UGH

23 Which word means the opposite of PERFUNCTORY?

a) VINDICATED
b) CAREFUL
c) HINDERED
d) FREAKISH
e) CANDID

24 What is HODOPHOBIA the fear of?

a) PINS
b) TRAVEL
c) PAIN
d) STARS
e) IDEAS

25 Rearrange these words to find a trite saying.

WAY	STRIKE	FLOOR	WILL
TOOL	ITS	FIRST	YOUR
ANY		ON	THE
FOOT	ALWAYS	TO	DROPPED

26 Fill in the blanks to make two words which are synonyms. You may move either clockwise or anticlockwise.

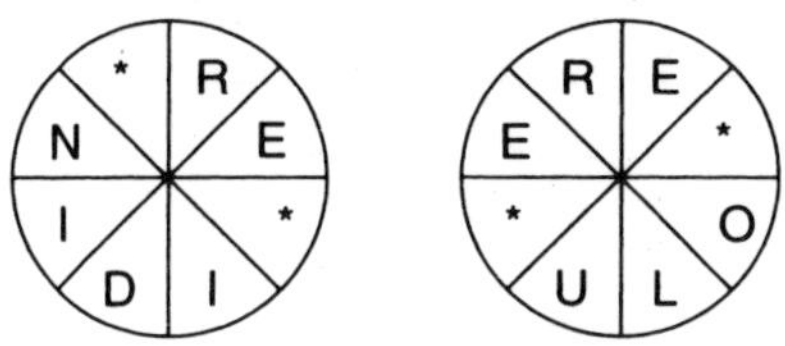

27 Each of the nine squares in the grid marked 1A to 3C should incorporate all the lines and symbols which are shown in the squares of the same letter and number immediately above and to the left. For example, 2B should incorporate all the lines and symbols that are in 2 and B.

One of the squares is incorrect. Which one is it?

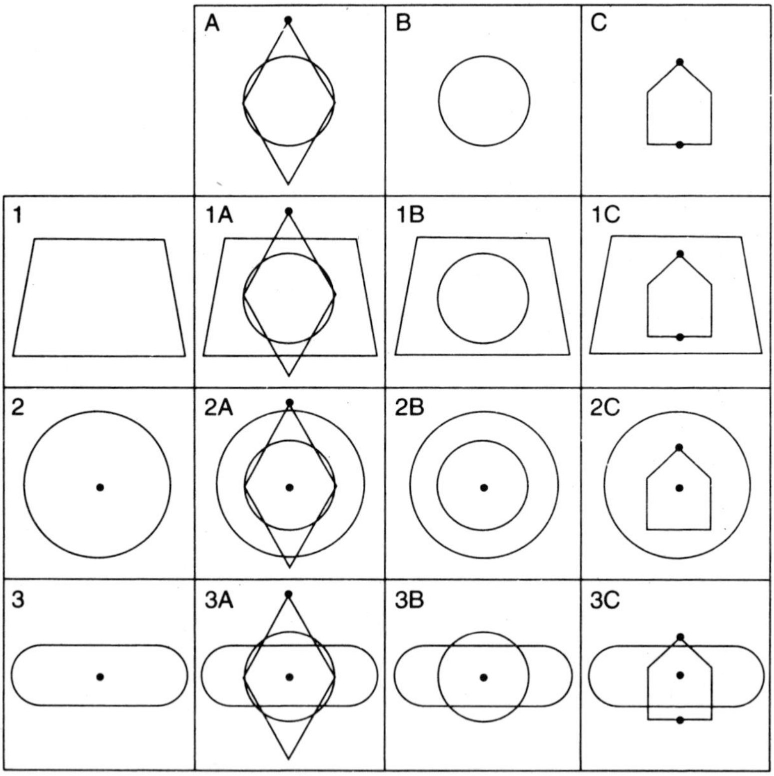

28 Simplify

$6 \times 10 - 2 \times 12 + 6$

29 Find a word which when placed in front of these words makes new words.

PLANE
TING
(. . .) SIDE
SHELL
WEED
GULL

30 Find a ten-letter word that is a bird.

. O . T . U . K . R

31 If 32 = 40 then 21 = ?

32 E – P = L
L + I = X
H – P = F
F – B = Y
X – C = A
I – A = O
C + W = ?

What is the value of ?

33 What does this mathematical sign mean?

$\gg$

a) much greater than
b) much less than
c) ratio to
d) not greater than
e) not equal to

34

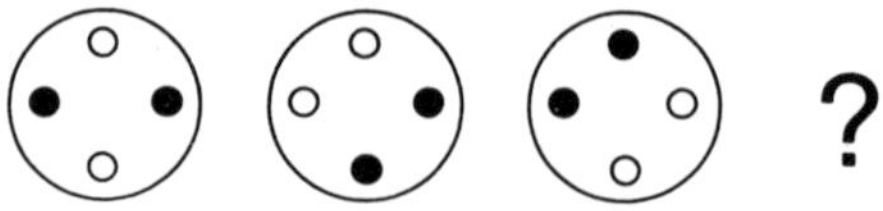

What comes next in the sequence?

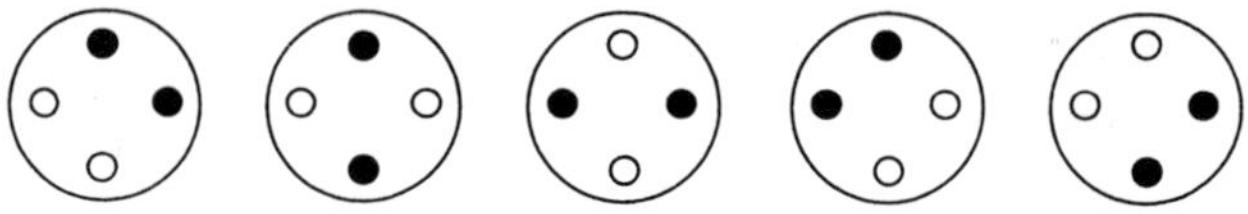

A B C D E

35 Find three countries.

. B . S . I . I .
. N . O . E . I .
. I . G . P . R .

36 Place two four-letter bits together to make an eight-letter vehicle.

ZKAR BARO STAR BRIT
RICK PUST DUSS SHAR
CART ROAD UCHE

37 OSTENTATION is to PEACOCKS as NIDE is to

a) PHEASANT
b) MARTENS
c) PENGUINS
d) SWALLOWS

38 What is always part of LINGUINI?

a) PASTA
b) LIQUORICE
c) STRAWBERRIES
d) LEMON CURD
e) YORKSHIRE PUDDING

39 Find a ten-letter word by travelling through the rooms in any order, but only go into each room once.

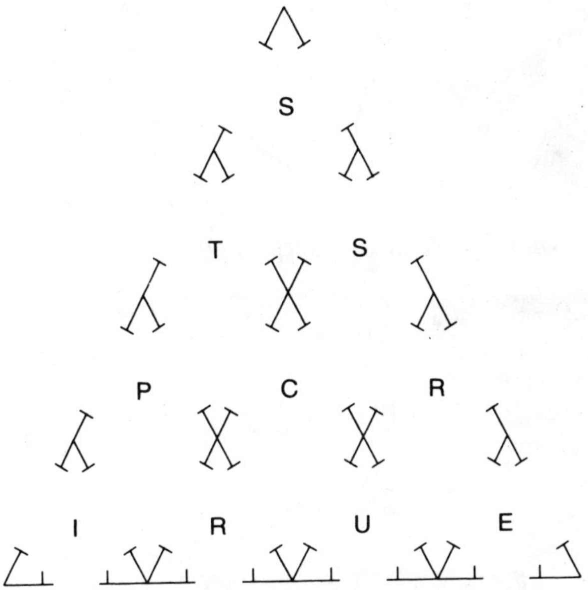

40 Which circle is the odd one out?

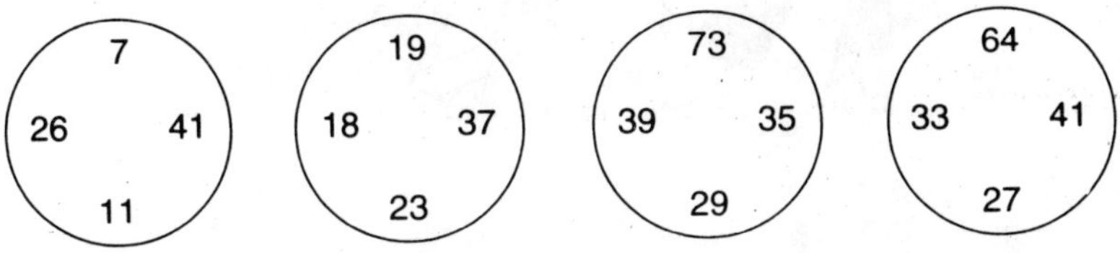

A B C D

Test ten

1

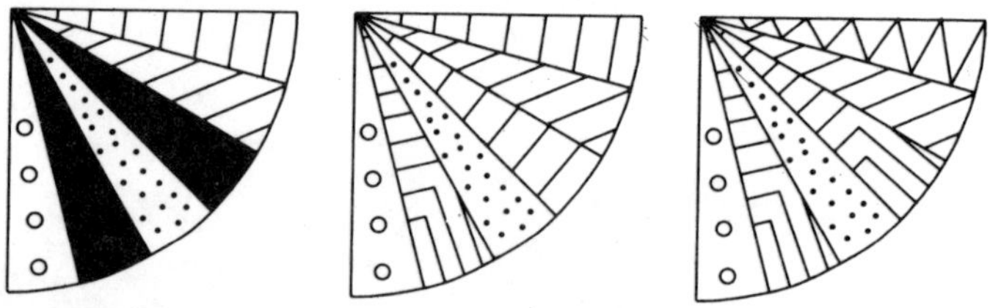

What comes next in this sequence?

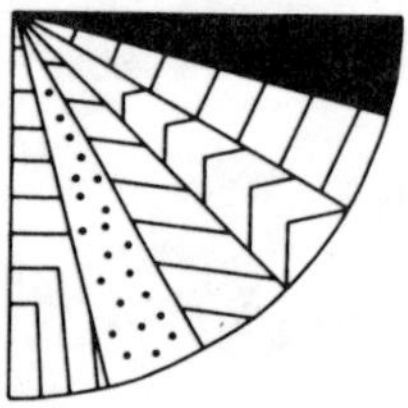

A

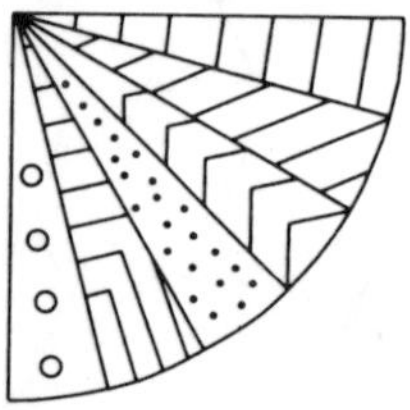

B

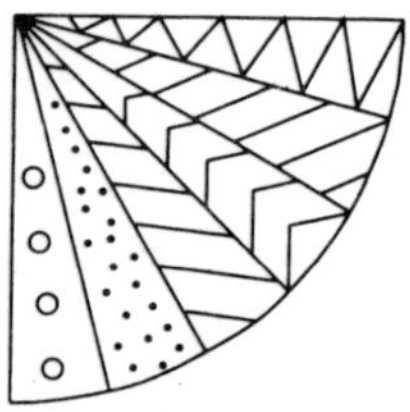

C

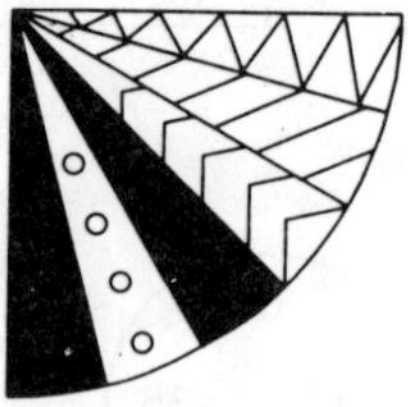

D

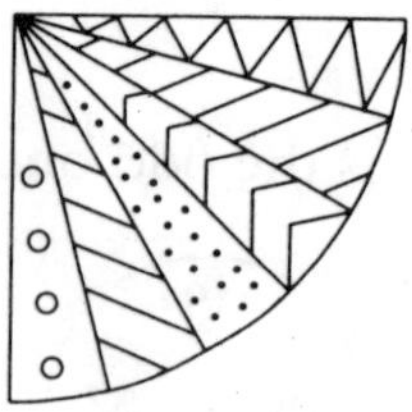

E

2 Harry is a third again as old as Dick, who is a third as old again as Tom. Their combined ages total 148. How old are the three men?

3 MANDIBLE is to JAWBONE as STERNUM is to:

a) CHEEKBONE
b) THIGHBONE
c) COLLARBONE
d) BREASTBONE
e) ANKLEBONE

4 Which group of letters is the odd one out?

HCI
LGA
EHCD
NBD
KIP
BOC
FAID

5. semi-circle, square, hexagon, ?

What comes next?

heptagon, pentagon, rectangle, decagon, octagon

6

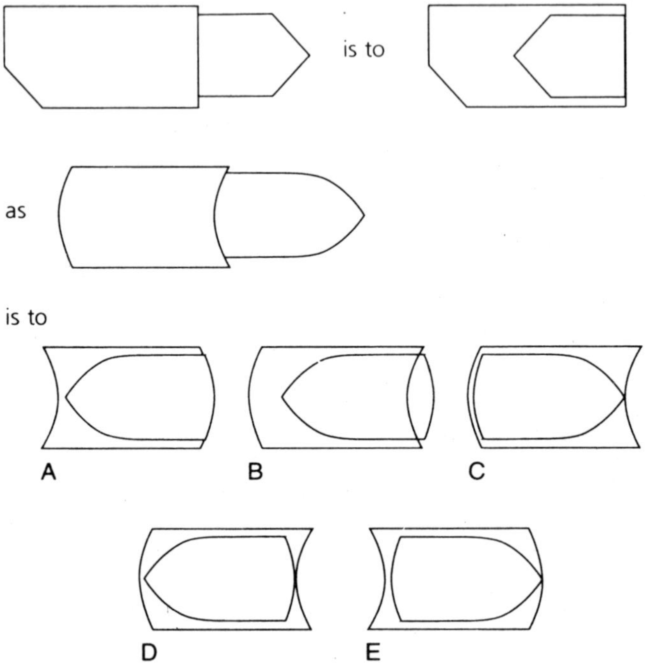

7 What do the following words have in common?

restaurant, altogether, flattery

8 Solve the anagrams to complete the quotation by Samuel Johnson.

(atom spirit) is the last refuge of a (cold nurse)

9 What is the meaning of PERFIDY?

a) loss of the soul
b) distrust
c) punishment
d) treachery
e) utopia

10 Decipher each anagram to find two phrases that are spelled differently but sound alike. For example, a name, an aim.

eager pat   page tyre

11 How many circles appear below:

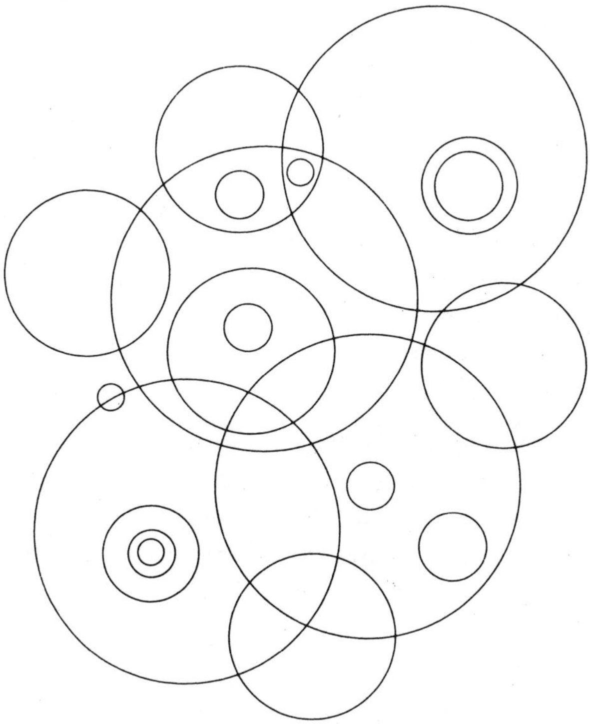

12 Find the starting point and move vertically or horizontally, but not diagonally to spell out a seventeen-letter phrase.

N	D	O		
E	E	V		
B	R	B	A	C
		A	W	K
		R	D	S

13 Which of these words is the odd one out?

a) FURNISHED
b) NUTSHELL
c) USHERETTE
d) REFRESHING
e) DISHEVELLED
f) ESTABLISHED

14 What is indicated below?

The first of October
A fifth of scotch
The tail of a rattlesnake
The centre of the hexagon
The end of autumn

15 A train travelling at a speed of 80 mph enters a tunnel that is 0.75 miles long. The length of the train is 0.25 miles. How long does it take for all of the train to pass through the tunnel, from the moment the front enters to the moment the rear emerges?

16 Add one letter, not necessarily the same letter, to each word in the front, end or middle to find two words that mean the same.

LEER RISE

17 The transpennine railway links Hull and Liverpool, which are 128 miles apart. A train leaves Hull travelling at 75 mph. Another train leaves Liverpool at exactly the same time travelling at 85 mph. Both trains are non-stop. Which train will be furthest from Hull when they meet?

18 Use each letter of the newspaper headline once each only to spell out three card games:

COW KICKS BATH PAL JERK

19 ARCH, EDGY, ?

Which word comes next?

PANG, INKY, LODE, ACID, COSY

20 Which is the odd one out?

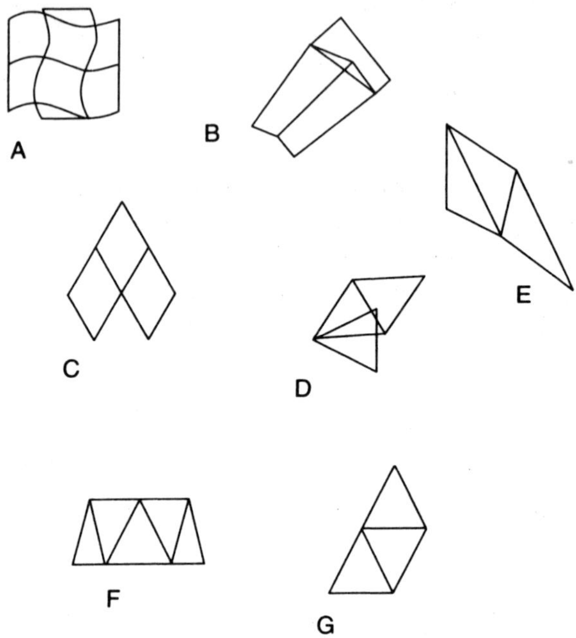

21 Simplify

$16 - 2 \times 2 + 10 \div 4$

22 Find an anagram of

HAS TO PILFER

A . . . .

There is a clue in the puzzle

23 Which two words mean the same?

MARSHAL, COMFORT, SAVOUR, AGITATE, OBSCURE, GATHER, DISJOIN

24 Find three insects.

. I . L . P . D .
. O . K . O . C .
. U . T . R . L .

25 This nine-letter word has been mixed up. See if you can untangle it.

S	E	R
E	M	E
T	U	K

26 Fill in the blanks, to find two words which are synonyms. You may move either clockwise or anticlockwise.

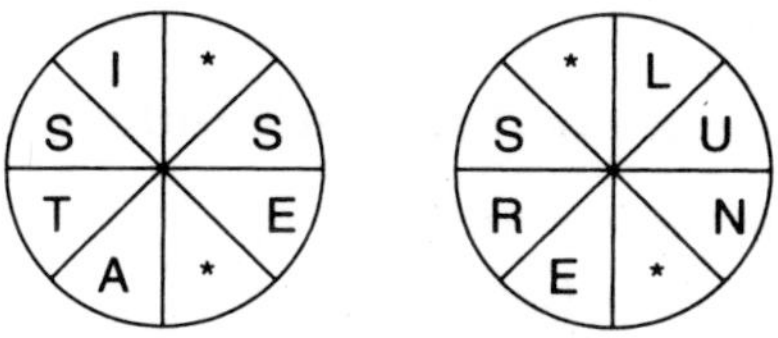

27

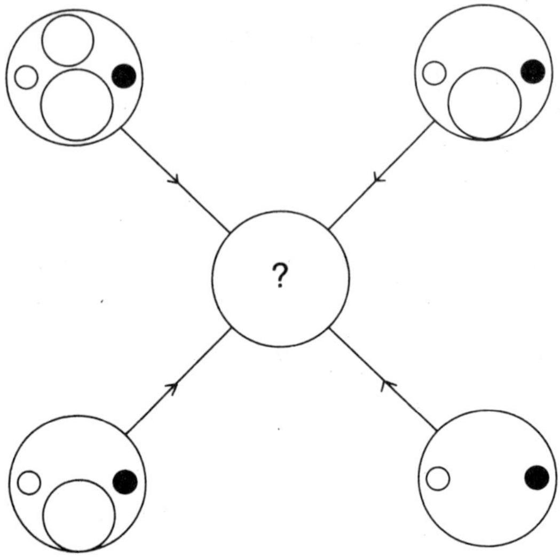

Each line and symbol which appears in the four outer circles, above is transferred to the centre circle according to these rules:

If a line or symbol occurs in the outer circles:

Once: it is transferred
Twice: it is possibly transferred
Three times: it is transferred
Four times: it is not transferred

Which of the circles shown below should appear at the centre of the diagram, above?

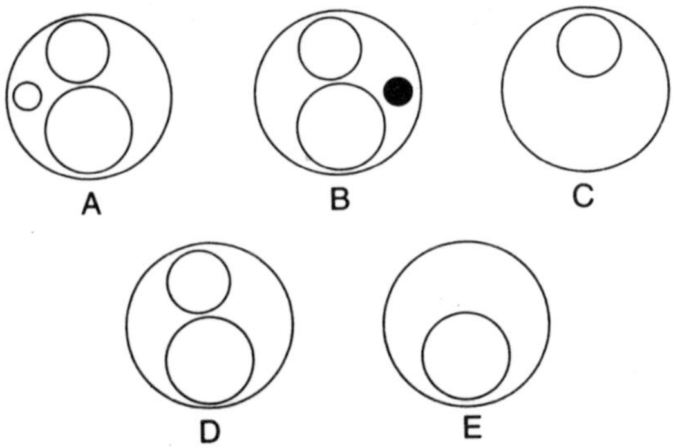

28 Find this eleven-letter word. It is a legal term.

. O . E . L . S . R .

29 Place two sets of three letters together to make a vegetable.

LEN	POT	ATE	TOM	ROT
LEC	TLE	ATE	GAR	CAR

30 Which of these anagrams is not a fruit?

a) RECHRY
b) CHYEEL
c) NAGORE
d) NIQCEU
e) DINGOI

31 What is ANTLOPHOBIA the fear of?

a) DOGS
b) FLOODS
c) TOUCH
d) DAWN
e) POISON

32 Which circle is the odd one out?

A

17	22
16	24
31	18

B

19	10
20	12
27	44

C

15	22
14	18
23	12

D

13	20
30	18
19	26

33 Fill in the blanks to find an eight-letter insect. You may move either clockwise or anticlockwise.

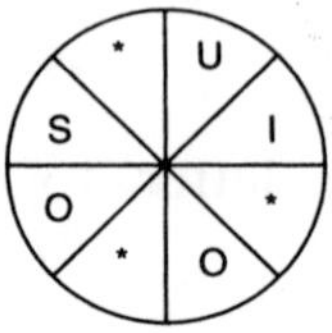

34 Which is the odd one out?

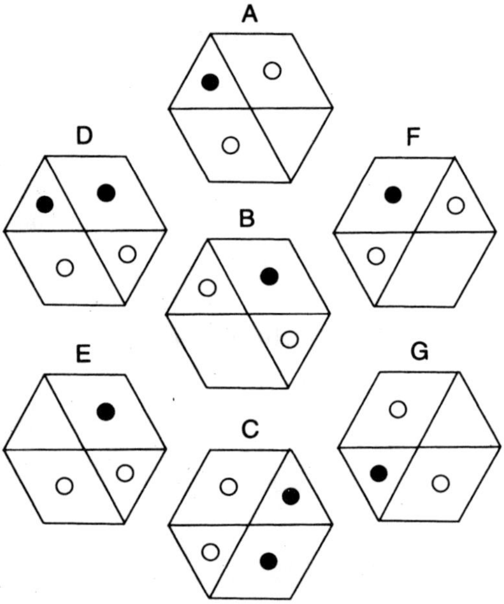

35 Find a ten-letter word which is a chemical.

. H . S . H . R . S

36 Find a word which when placed on the end of these words makes new words.

COLD
MILD
KIND (. . . .)
FAIR
POLITE

37 What is always part of to NICTATE?

a) ANGULAR VELOCITY
b) FINGER
c) EAR
d) EYELID
e) TONGUE

38 Find a ten-letter word which is an animal.

. A . E . O . A . D

39 Which word when placed in front of these words makes new words?

BAKED
BRED
(. . . .) CROWN
DOZEN
FACE

40 What does this mathematical sign mean?

$\equiv$

a) identical with
b) equals
c) proportionate to
d) greater than
e) less than

Answers

Test one

1 B; only when a dot appears in the same position once in the first three circles is it carried forward to the final circle.

2 ESPLANADE; all the others are stretches of water.

3 20, 7; to obtain the numbers in the larger segments, add the two numbers to the right and multiply the two numbers to the left.

4 TEND; the consonants N D L T are being repeated in the same order.

5 C; looking across and down, each row and column should have one of each eye type and curl type, i.e. left, right and centre.

6 77; $13 \times 9 = 117$, $11 \times 7 = 77$

7 HUMILITY

8 the buck stops here

9 PLEASURE

10 d) a person converted to a religion

11 STORED
PA (ST) UN
MO (OR) AL
BR (ED) IT

12 8 7
4 6

The numbers 487625 are being repeated in the pattern shown

4	8	7	6	2	5	4	8
5	7	8	2	6	4	5	7
2	6	4	5	7	8	2	6
6	2	5	4	**8**	**7**	6	2
7	5	2	8	**4**	**6**	7	5
8	4	6	7	5	2	8	4
4	8	7	6	2	5	4	8

13 D; in all the others the arrow is pointing to the curved side.

14 4; looking at the two arrays of numbers, in the second array the numbers in the top line reduce by 1 from the first array, in the second line they increase by 1, and in the third line they reduce by 1.

15 F

16 ESCALATE

17 D; the figure rotates by 90° and the patterns change to different corners according to the first analogy.

18 MERCA = cream

19 penitent, remorseless

20 e) ANTI-CLOCKWISE

21 e) REITERATION

22 FLOORER

23 BASILISK

24 ORCHESTRA

25 CLOISTERED

26 MONGOOSE

27 2C

28 b) VEXATION

29 WHALER, LUGGER

30 12; there are two series, +7 and – 6:
+7: 1, 8, 15, 22
– 6: 30, 24, 18, 12

31 FEASIBLE, IMPRACTICABLE

32 EXPLICITNESS

33 8
6 + 14 = 20, 20 ÷ 5 = 4
8 + 4 = 12, 12 ÷ 2 = 6
9 + 16 = 25, 25 ÷ 5 = 5
7 + 7 = 14, 14 ÷ 2 = 7
4 + 4 = 8, 8 ÷ 1 = 8

34 LORDSHIP, ASSIGNEE, CANNULAR

35 NEGLIGENCE

36 GALAPAGOS
MANHATTAN
NANTUCKET

37 $\frac{123.654}{999}$

1 = .123777
1000 = 123.777777
999 = 123.654

38 $\frac{1}{2}$

$16 - (9 \times 2) + (5 \div 2) =$

$16 - 18 + 2\frac{1}{2} = \frac{1}{2}$

$(\times, \div)$ must be evaluated before $(+, -)$

39 NORTHAMPTONSHIRE

40 IMAGINED, SPURIOUS

Test two

1 D; at each stage the figure rotates through 90° clockwise and the dot moves to a different segment in turn.

2 a) SHAPELESS

3 The final column should contain the numbers. 4, 24, 124, 624. The numbers in the first column progress $\times 2 + 1$, in the second column they progress $\times 3 + 2$, in the third column they progress $\times 4 + 3$ and in the fourth column they progress $\times 5 + 4$.

4 ANNEAL

5. F; the contents of the final square in each row and column are determined by the contents of the first two squares. Lines from these first two squares are carried forward to the third square unless the same line appears in both squares, in which case it is cancelled out.

6 146; reverse the numbers each side of the brackets and take the difference: 569 – 423 = 146.

7 RECONCILE

8 UNGRACIOUS, CIVIL

9 T; letters in alternate opposite segments are the same distance from the beginning and end of the alphabet respectively, i.e. C and X are three places from the beginning and end of the alphabet, respectively, etc.

10 IRONY, SATIRE

11 A; split the row into groups of four symbols. At each stage a symbol is shaded moving left to right then back to the front again.

12 2; the sums of the numbers in the larger bottom segments are half the sum of the numbers in their corresponding segment in the top half. So, 9 + 7 + 8 = 24 and 9 + 1 + 2 = 12. The sum of the numbers in the smaller segments top and bottom are the same.

13 Cool van = volcano. The countries are Poland (old pan), Belgium (big mule), Norway (any row) and Hungary (hay rung)

14 Monday

15 ET; they are the last two letters of the colours of the rainbow; red, orange, yellow, green, blue, indigo, violet.

16 PERTAIN, APPLY

17 B; the ends of the five lines terminate at the corners of a hexagon.

18 They all contain sea-going vessels: ark, gig, tug, brig

19 slip of the pen

20 7

	8		(7)	
			6	
9			3	

21 CARICATURE

22 .7692

23 ATAXIA

24 MADONNA
FAIRBANKS
STREISAND

25 EYESIGHT, LOVEBIRD

26 OUTBREAK, ERUPTION

27 C

28 CHLOROFORM

29 COLLIE

30 e) SERIOUS

31 FATHOM, ANCHOR

32 If computers get too powerful we can organise them into committees, that will do them in.

33 B; the three are SCAMPI, SCARAB, SCANTY

34 3C

35 d) a four-wheeled carriage

36 a) COWARDICE

37 $3\frac{3}{4}$; there are two series: $+1\frac{1}{4}$ and $-2\frac{3}{4}$
$+1\frac{1}{4}$: $2\frac{1}{2}$, $3\frac{3}{4}$, 5, $6\frac{1}{4}$
$-2\frac{3}{4}$: 12, $9\frac{1}{4}$, $6\frac{1}{2}$, $3\frac{3}{4}$

38 PENITENTIARY

39 MANIFOLD

40 WARBLE-FLY

WOOD-LOUSE

Test three

1 STALEMATE

2 5; each line of numbers contains the digits 1–9 once each only.

3 on second thoughts

4 47; take the square root of each pair of digits, i.e. 16 (4), 49 (7)

5 B; in all the others the dot is inside the circle.

6 R(OMAN)IA

7 BELFRY; it is at the top of the church, all the others are at ground level.

8 SOPORIFIC, SLEEPY

9 E; in all the others the black dot is on the outside of the three connected dots. In E it is in the middle.

10 10; the numbers on the outside are the sum of the numbers in the two adjoining segments plus the number in the middle.

11 Grover Cleveland

12 DEATHLESS, EPHEMERAL

13 ORDINARY, STANDARD

14 MARSH, SWAMP

15 C; the rest are the same figure rotated.

16 6; 72 × 3 = 216

17 a) HARE

18 E; take the six letters in the same position in each group of four letters to spell out the words ABSENT, BAFFLE, CRAFTY, DIVIDE.

19 PERSONAL COMPUTER

20 F; there are three different arrows, the arrows move 45° clockwise at each stage and alternate white/black.

21 $\frac{7}{13}$

$$\frac{7}{13} \times 4 = \frac{28}{52} \times 9 = \frac{252}{468} \times 5 = \frac{1260}{2340}$$

22 c) FLABBY

23 PEERAGE

24 ELECTRIFY, TRANQUILLISE

25 UNSEEMLY, SUITABLE

26 CLEMENTINE

27 K E, above the line; CO, below the line; letters formed only of straight lines are above the line, those with curved lines are below.

28 ROOKS

29 BASNET, CUDGEL

30 BECHAMEL

31 If ambition doesn't hurt you haven't got it

32 FLAMETHROWER

33 LITERATE, IGNORANT

34 SHARKSKINS

35 c) RED

36 MINNOW

37 a) pertaining to CROSSROADS

38 DIMINUENDO

39 KINGSHIP, JEWELLER

40 3

$9 \div 3 = 3, \quad 3 - 2 = 1$

$24 \div 2 = 12, \quad 12 - 6 = 6$

$21 \div 3 = 7, \quad 7 - 4 = 3$

$18 \div 3 = 6, \quad 6 - 4 = 2$

$20 \div 5 = 4, \quad 4 - 1 = 3$

Test four

1 A; move from letter to letter in the following sequence: A(B)C(DEF)G(H)I(JKL)M(N)O(PQR)S(T)U(VWX)Y(Z)A(B CD)E(F)G

2 EMPIRICAL

3 c) DASH

4 8; looking both across and down, each pair of numbers totals one more than the previous pair of numbers, so 8 + 3 = 11 and 4 + 8 = 12.

5 E; the rectangle turns to a circle and the circles within the figure move to different positions as in the original analogy.

6 55; following the path shown below, each number is the sum of the previous two numbers.

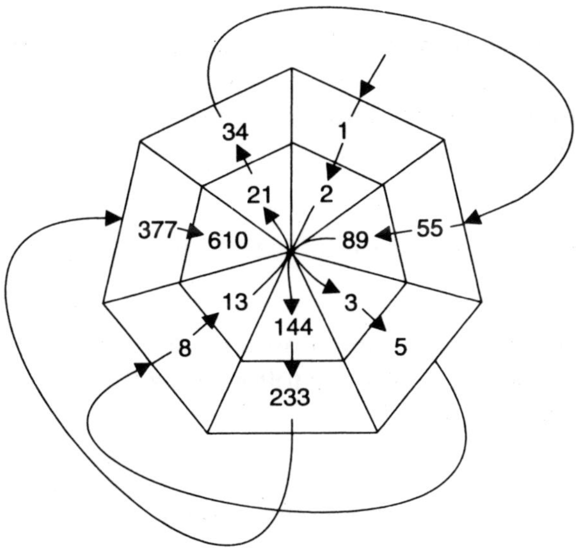

7 GAINSAY, CONTRADICT

8 ESCAPOLOGIST

9 UNINFORMED

10 CUPBOARD

11 B; the rectangle moves through 90° and goes inside the square, which increases in size. The bullet turns 180° and goes at the bottom.

12 70; start at 1 and move clockwise to alternate segments, adding 4, 7, 10, 13, 16, 19, i.e. the amount added increases by 3 each time.

13 A; start at the letter C second from left on the top row and, working anti-clockwise via the middle letter and jumping to alternate letters, spell out the word CIRCUMNAVIGATOR.

14 XYZ = ART: artery, parted, hearth, thwart

15 9731842; take the original number and arrange the odd digits in descending order followed by the even digits in descending order.

16 C; straight lines turn to circles and circles to straight lines.

17 LAG

18 SHOOT/CHUTE

19 RATED
ALONE
TOAST
ENSUE
DETER

20 A; the number of triangles produced by the figures increases by one each time.

21 c) PLUMP

22 OOLOGY

23 c) TARKEA (KARATE)

The others are: CUPOLA, GARRET, PLINTH, GIRDER

24 a) NATURAL

25 LOLLYPOP, LYREBIRD

26 FLOUNDER

27 B

28 $\frac{7}{8}$

$$\frac{7}{8} \times 3 = \frac{21}{24} \times 7 = \frac{147}{168} \times 10 = \frac{1470}{1680}$$

29 SALVIA

30 CHISEL, GIMLET

31 GINGIVITIS

32 RING

33 D; the others are A QUOITS, B QUOTES, C QUORUM

34 A

35 CHICKADEE
BUFFALO
TAPIR

36 a) PERT SPEECH

37 3.4; there are two series, +0.9 and – 0.9
+ 0.9: 2.2, 3.1, 4.0, 4.9
– 0.9: 6.1, 5.2, 4.3, 3.4

38 0.5333

39 The only way to compensate for the shortness of life is to wear a long face.

40 343; starting at 1 and jumping two segments each time, the numbers 1 to 8 are cubed, giving the following sequence:

Number:	1	2	3	4	5	6	7	8
Cubed:	1	8	27	64	125	216	343	512

Test five

1 15

2 4817 and 1387; the remaining numbers are in anagram pairs, one in the top circle and one in the bottom:

7496/9674, 2831/8132, 6279/7296, 3489/4398, 2614/4216.

3 3; the total of the numbers in each suit is 15.

4 DRESS

5 like a cat on a hot tin roof

6 ASS; the first and last letters are symbols of the chemical elements in alphabetical order, i.e. actinium (Ac), aluminium (Al), americium (Am), antimony (Sb), argon (Ar), arsenic (As).

7 careful, cautious, reticent, suspicious

8 a) HONEYCOMBED

9 F; a symbol moves from top to bottom in turn, first the bell and now the star. While it is moving it is shaded black.

10 PSEUDONYM

11 SPECULATOR

12 May; start by not missing any month, then miss one month, then two, then three etc.

13 6 2
3 4

The numbers 13426 are being repeated in the pattern shown below:

1	3	4	2	6	1	3
2	4	3	1	6	2	4
6	1	3	4	2	6	1
4	3	1	**6**	**2**	4	3
2	6	1	**3**	**4**	2	6
3	1	6	2	4	3	1
4	2	6	1	3	4	2

14 FRAGMENT

15 84; start at 7 and work down the left-hand column × 3 + 1, and down the right-hand column × 2 + 4.

16 D; only when a symbol appears in the same position in the first two squares of a row or column is it carried forward to the third square.

17 AVATAR

18 faithful, disloyal

19 sulky

20 C; its symbols appear in the same order as the others but travel round in the opposite direction.

21 INVIOLABLE, SACROSANCT

22 TATTERS

23 d) GHIDNY (DINGHY); the others are gullet, larynx, fibula, kidney.

24 AGE

25 33 $6 \times 4 = 24, 24 - 3 = 21$
$8 \times 8 = 64, 64 - 2 = 62$
$7 \times 3 = 21, 21 - 10 = 11$
$8 \times 3 = 24, 24 - 5 = 19$
$7 \times 5 = 35, 35 - 2 = 33$

26 CHEERFUL, MOURNFUL

27 2B

28 40; 55 in base 9 = 50, 44 in base 9 = 40

29 LARKS

30 a) EAGER

31 The dimmer the light the greater the scandal

32 HAEMOPHILIAC

33 PERIWINKLE

34 B; A represents even numbers, B represents square numbers, C represents odd numbers.

35 $\frac{6}{11}$

36 PLAICE

37 INSENSIBLE, TEMPERATE

38 c) WOMEN

39 I; letters in the top row are the same distance from the beginning of the alphabet as those in the bottom row are from the end, i.e. C and X are three places from the beginning and the end of the alphabet, respectively.

40 BANDICOOT

Test six

1 FRACTION

2 OCCUPATIONAL

3 line of least resistance

4 ARGUE

5 B: everything on the outside goes to the inside and vice versa; black circles turn to white triangles and vice versa, and white circles turn to black triangles and vice versa.

6 9; 27568321 + 49371572 = 76939893 and 76939893 + 18476238 = 95416131

7 disturb, bother

8 9; 27 ÷ 9 = 3, similarly 28 ÷ 4 = 7.

9 C; each connected line of three circles contains one each of the three symbols.

10 c) the shore

11 ALTOGETHER

12 3246; in all the others multiply the first and last digits together to obtain the middle two digits.

13 JUBILATE

14 The final column should contain the numbers 3858. There are four sequences of numbers following the route shown below.

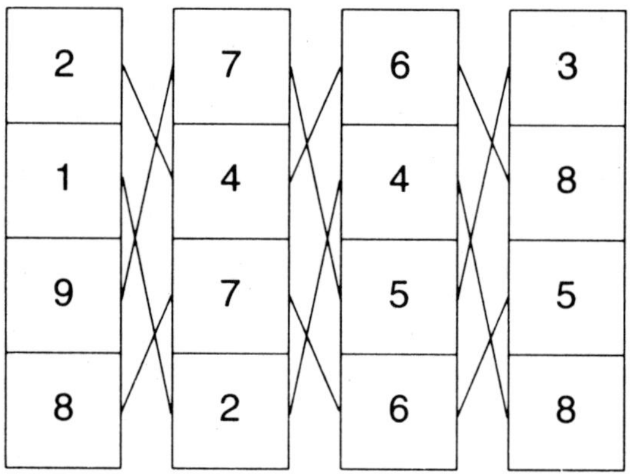

15 E; A and D are the same with black and white reversal, as are C and B.

16 needle PI (NE) CK
SH (ED) IT
SO (LE) AN

17 least/leased

18 14313

19 b) ROISTERING

20 A; to complete every possible pairing of the four different symbols.

21 HELIOTROPE

22 PORBEAGLE
SWORDFISH
TRUMPETER

23 WEASEL

24 EUCALYPTUS

25 INCUBATE, JUBILANT

26 TIDINESS, DISORDER

27 C

28 a) SORD

29 e) RECTIFICATION

30 STEPPE

31 6.28; there are two series: – 0.06 and +0.06
– 0.06: 6.72, 6.66, 6.60, 6.54
+ 0.06: 6.10, 6.16, 6.22, 6.28

32 PROVINCES

33 B; the other are: A yoicks, C yogurt, D yonder.

34 DISCOVERED

35 0.9444

36 $\frac{9}{14}$

$$\frac{9}{14} \times 6 = \frac{54}{84} \times 7 = \frac{378}{588} \times 5 = \frac{1890}{2940}$$

37 ABSINTHE

38 IMBROGLIO, COMPLEXITY

39 SPONGE

40 INTERIORS

Test seven

1 D; so that each line and column contains one of the four different symbols.

2 7; 784 ÷ 7 = 112

3 RARE PLENTIFUL

4 GRIEVANCE

5 23 minutes

6 MOBILE

7 A; only when a dot appears in the same position in three of the surrounding circles is it transferred to the centre circle.

8 laudable, unworthy

9 encouragement (one cute German). Disarray is an anagram indicator; reassurance is the definition.

10. V
T
W
U

The four consecutive letters of the alphabet are placed in the same order as in the previous two columns.

11 15; 45 + 30 = 75, 75 ÷ 15 = 5

12 latent talent

13 They all have a country embedded in them:

TAX(I RAN)K
GLOS(S PAIN)T
T(OM AN)D JERRY

14 B; all the others are the same box rotated.

15 ADRIENNE; an anagram of RAIN NEED.

16 8; numbers in the same position in both figures add up to 10.

17 MULBERRY; to give him, flu, pal, tab, see, mar, bar and may.

18 NOISE; all the other words are in pairs where the last two letters of one word start the second word: lucid/diced, spare/erase, guile/elite, court/trust, irons/snore.

19 CONDUCTOR

20 B; the total number of sides of all the other pairs of figures is 11.

21 2; the number represents the number of ends that a letter has, e.g. E = 3.

22 PILLION

23 c) SNOW

24 HIPPODROME

25 30 $20 - 8 = 12,\ 12 \times 2 = 24$
$17 - 9 = 8,\ 8 \times 3 = 24$
$16 - 7 = 9,\ 9 \times 4 = 36$
$9 - 6 = 3,\ 3 \times 5 = 15$
$8 - 3 = 5,\ 5 \times 6 = 30$

26 KOOKABURRA

27 2B

28 If someone says I'm expensive, they will be

29 DAMSON

30 e) ROWHAR (HARROW); the others are: escudo, nickel, rouble, shekel.

31 FLORID, FLUSHED

32 ANAESTHETIST

33 CAREFREE, WATCHFUL

34 22

35 – 11; $6 - (7 \times 3) + (8 \div 2) = 6 - 21 + 4 = -11$
($\times$, $\div$) must be evaluated before (+, –)

36 CONVERSATION

37 CROWS

38 b) LOOP

39 a) plus or minus

40 A; all of the circles contain prime numbers except A (39).

Test eight

1 C; the top two symbols turn upside down and move to the bottom. One dot goes in the middle figure and two in the bottom figure.

2 1 a.m.

3 CARMINE; it is red, the rest are black.

4 PLEASE, DISGUST

5 3; it is the number of straight lines in the three letters.

6 SUBORDINATE; the number of letters increases by two each time and another vowel is added, a, ae, aei, aeio, aeiou.

7 30; add the percentages together, 87 + 79 + 68 + 96 = 330. Divide by 3, which gives 100 with three items and 30 left over having all four items.

8 A; the left half moves to the right and the right half to the left.

9 A KRONA = ANORAK; the sports are baseball (all babes), archery (hear cry), karate (a taker) and lacrosse (lose cars).

10 R; start at T, top left, and move to alternate letters. When reaching the end of the bottom row move to the E next to the T on the top row and start the process again. The phrase THROW A SPANNER IN THE WORKS will be spelled out.

11 If marriage were outlawed, only outlaws would have inlaws.

12 PIGEON, MAGPIE, TURKEY

13 512943; the numbers move as follows:

ABCDEF EBFADC
913452 512943

14 SUB; the letters of each word move forward three places in the alphabet.

15 SIGHING

16 SAUCEPAN: to give has, pea, you, arc, cue, rap, lea, pen.

17 Sid 36, Jim 54, Alf 81.

18 7; look along identical sections in each circle to find four sequences: 7531, 4567, 9876, 1357.

19 B; the top half drops onto the bottom half and the previously black figures become white and transparent.

20 It is better to have a permanent income than to be fascinating.

Humility is no substitute for a good personality.

The English instinctively admire any man who has no talent and is modest about it.

21 CORMORANT
GOLDFINCH
STONECHAT

22 SORROW

23 d) FASHIONABLE

24 c) FOLDING TOP

25 SONG

26 CALLIPERS

27 A

28 45

20 (base 10) = 32 (base 6) $(3 \times 6) + (2 \times 1)$
29 (base 10) = 45 (base 6) $(4 \times 6) + (5 \times 1)$

29 WILLOW

30 HELPMATE, ADVERSARY

31 JUGGERNAUT

32 e) not greater than

33 B; ENZYME, ENGULF, ENGAGE

34 ONAGER, OUTLAW, SALLOW

35 – 62; $6 - 10 \times 2 - 12 \times 4 = 6 - 20 - 48 = 62$
$(\times, \div)$ must be evaluated before $(+, -)$

36 PARLIAMENT

37 MIDSHIPMAN

38 b) CHARLATAN

39 D; all circles add to 100 except D = 99.

40 BOBOLINK

Test nine

1 D: all lines in opposite segments rotate 90°.

2 231

3 GOODBYE, FAREWELL

4 head to head

5 clutch

6 C; it only contains one white dot, the others contain two.

7 LUDGE = glued

8 MCK; the letters CKLM are being repeated in the pattern shown below.

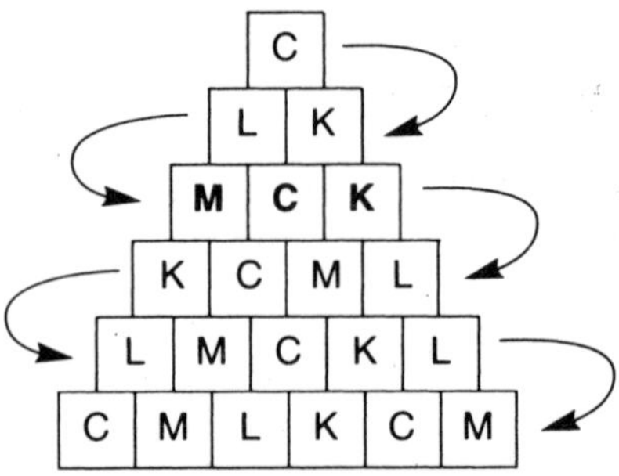

9 16

10 procrastinate (satanic report)

11 It enables you to spell the word MNEMONICS correctly by taking the first letter of each word.

12 I, in, sin, sing, using, musing, amusing OR I, in, sin, sing, sting, siting, smiting.

13 remote meteor

14 D; it spirals clockwise, the rest spiral anticlockwise.

15 23 tomatoes into 19 bags. 437 is the product of two prime numbers, 19 and 23. The smaller of these two numbers is the number of bags, as you wish to use the smallest number of bags possible.

16 Work to the pattern shown below, missing an extra space between letters each time.

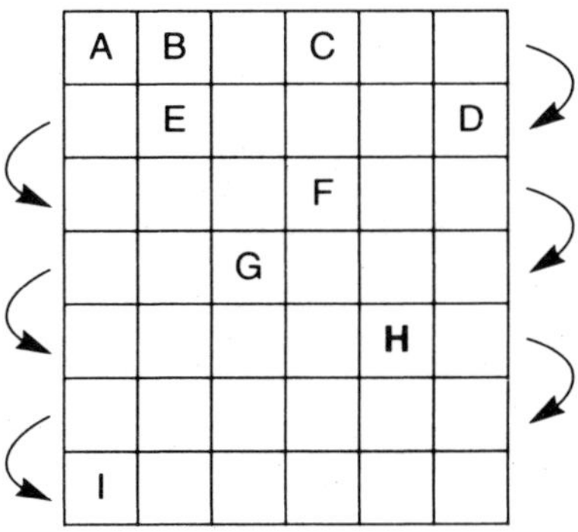

17 ravine

18 Visit the squares in the order shown below:

5	7	2
8	1	4
3	T	6

19 47 socks: if he takes out 45 socks, although it is a long shot, they could be all the blue socks and all the red socks. To be 100% certain he has a pair of grey socks he must take out two more.

20 C; each time two symbols touch they are replaced by two different symbols.

21 The best way to break a habit is to drop it.

22 CHOUGH

23 b) CAREFUL

24 b) TRAVEL

25 On its way to the floor, any dropped tool will always first strike your foot.

26 INTREPID, RESOLUTE

27 2C

28 42; $6 \times 10 - 2 \times 12 + 6 = 60 - 24 + 6 = 42$
($\times$, $\div$) must be evaluated before (+, –)

29 SEA

30 GOATSUCKER

31 25

32 (base 10) = 40 (base 8) (4×8)
21 (base 10) = 25 (base 8) $(2 \times 8) + (5 \times 1)$

32 X; numbers are end points of lines: B = 0, X = 4, Y = 3, C = 2 etc.

33 a) much greater than

34 C

35 ABYSSINIA
INDONESIA
SINGAPORE

36 BAROUCHE

37 PHEASANTS

38 a) PASTA

39 SCRIPTURES

40 D; it contains a square number, $64 = 8^2$.

Test ten

1 E; when identical segments appear in a figure they are replaced by two new and different segments at the next stage.

2 Tom 36, Dick 48, Harry 64.

3 BREASTBONE

4 KIP; taking the numerical position of each letter in the alphabet, all the other groups of letters total 20. KIP totals 36.

5 octagon; the numbers of sides in the figures increases by two each time.

6 D; the smaller figure flips into the larger figure.

7 They all begin with musical terms: rest, alto, flat.

8 Patriotism is the last refuge of a scoundrel.

9 d) TREACHERY

10 great ape, grey tape

11 20

12 bend over backwards

13 refreshing; all other words have SHE embedded in them.

14 The word OCEAN; i.e. the first letter of October is O, the fifth letter of scotch is C, etc.

15 45 seconds; $(0.75 + 0.25) \times \frac{60}{80}$.

16 LEVER, PRISE

17 No calculations are necessary. Obviously the trains will be both the same distance from Hull when they meet, and they will both be the same distance from Liverpool.

18 poker, blackjack, whist

19 inky; alternate letters are alternate letters of the alphabet; ArCh, EdGy, InKy.

20 F; all the others are made up from three identical figures. F is made up from just two parallelograms.

21 $14\frac{1}{2}$; $16 - 2 \times 2 + 10 \div 4 = 16 - 4 + 2\frac{1}{2} = 14\frac{1}{2}$
$(\times, \div)$ must be evaluated before $(+, -)$

22 A SHOPLIFTER

23 MARSHAL, GATHER

24 MILLIPEDE
COCKROACH
BUTTERFLY

25 MUSKETEER

26 MISTAKES, BLUNDERS

27 D

28 FORECLOSURE

29 CARROT

30 DINGOI (INDIGO); the others are cherry, lychee, orange, quince.

31 b) FLOODS

32 D; in A, B and C the left-hand three numbers = the right-hand total; D does not.

33 MOSQUITO

34 E

35 PHOSPHORUS

36 NESS

37 d) EYELID

38 CAMELOPARD (an old name for giraffe).

39 HALF

40 a) identical with